Encounters

How Racism Came to Ireland

Bill Rolston and Michael Shannon

First published 2002
by
Beyond the Pale
BTP Publications Ltd
Unit 2.1.2 Conway Mill
5-7 Conway Street
Belfast BT13 2DE

Tel: +44 (0)28 90 438630
Fax: +44 (0)28 90 439707
E-mail: office@btpale.com
Website: http://www.btpale.com

British Library Cataloguing-in-Publication Data.
A catalogue record for this book is available from the British Library.

ISBN 1-900960-15-X

Printed in Dublin by Colour Books Ltd.

Cover Photo: Neil Jarman. For an explanation of the banner, see page 64.
Portrait of Olaudah Equiano (page 3) reproduced by kind permission of
Royal Albert Memorial Museum, Exeter, Devon and the Bridgeman Art
Library, London.

Contents

For Michael and our family in Offaly.
And in memory of B.A.

Acknowledgements

Thanks for support and clues to: Martyn Anglesea, Ulster Museum, Belfast; Pat Benson, Sailortown Residents' Association, Belfast; Paul Burns, Belfast; Nicholas Canny, University College, Galway; Daniel Cassidy, San Francisco; Carol Coulter, Dublin; Michael Gorman, University of Ulster, Jordanstown; Desmond Fitzgerald, the Knight of Glin, Limerick; Olivia Fitzpatrick, Arts College, Belfast; Bill Hart, University of Ulster, Coleraine; Neil Jarman, Belfast; Keith Jeffery, University of Ulster, Jordanstown; Patricia Lundy, University of Ulster, Jordanstown; Seamus Mac Mathuna, University of Ulster, Coleraine; John Marshall, County Antrim; Karen McElrath, Queen's University, Belfast; Hector McDonnell, County Antrim; Madeleine Murray, Belfast; Jane Ohlmeyer, University of Aberdeen; Lord O'Neill, Shane's Castle, County Antrim; Nini Rodgers, Queen's University, Belfast; Mike Tomlinson, Queen's University, Belfast; Larry Walsh, Limerick Museum; Robert Welch, University of Ulster, Coleraine

1. Introduction

Towards the end of the 20th century the issue of racism came to the fore in Ireland, north and south. As refugees and asylum seekers from Africa, eastern Europe and elsewhere arrived in Dublin, a veritable moral panic emerged. Despite the fact that the number of such immigrants was remarkably small – in the late 1990s, more Irish people emigrated to the United States each year than the total number of immigrants in Ireland – the mass media partly articulated and partly enflamed popular fears about foreigners stealing jobs and houses from local people. Poorly thought-out government policies, such as dispersing asylum seekers to small towns in places like Kerry and Donegal, contributed to a growth of racist rhetoric. In such a climate, it was inevitable that vicious racist attacks would soon become part of the urban scene in Dublin. In this way, the Celtic tiger clearly revealed that it was no less a part of modern Europe than London, Rostock or Marseilles.

Nor were such racist attacks confined to newly arrived Africans and Europeans. The Chinese community had been well-established in the North for decades, with a growing number of second and even third-generation ethnic Chinese people in places like Belfast. Attacks on this community increased in the 1990s.

Even though the Lord Mayor of Belfast, Sammy Wilson, was able to state confidently in December 2000 that these attacks were to be explained in terms of robbery – as solely economic in origin[1] – it was clear to those at the receiving end that racism was central to the increase of robberies and the level of violence, including murder.

Many Irish people saw such racism as being new, out of character for Irish society, and practically inexplicable. The image of 'Ireland of the welcomes' had been irrevocably tarnished. A country which, per capita, had sent more emigrants to Britain, North America and elsewhere than any other, and ought therefore to have been able to empathise with others so displaced, seemed incapable of making the connections. How was this insensitivity to be explained? One popular explanation laid the blame on the phenomenon of migration itself: racism has increased because the number of immigrants has increased (for a critique, see McVeigh, 1998). This rationalisation has much in common with racism elsewhere, switching the blame from the behaviour of the host society to the single fact of the emigrants' presence; the migrant's crime is simply that of arrival in the host country (Webber, 1996).

A slightly more liberal approach is to acknowledge the racism of the host, but to explain it as due to 'teething problems'. Ireland is and has been a remarkably homogenous society; the Irish are not used to foreigners, especially black people; in time, familiarity will breed tolerance. Apart from the naïve optimism involved in this prediction, the explanation does not hold in the face of the historical record. The Irish have been encountering people of colour from at least the time of the Vikings. They have had more than enough time to 'get used' to black migrants. The fact that they have not yet done so derives from the uneven power relations involved in many of these encounters. Though racialised themselves, the Irish have often met black people in situations where they, the Irish, have had relative social, economic or political advantage. The roots of Irish racism are in the history of those uneven power relations.

The purpose of this account is to examine that history. We will look at the opportunities the Irish have had to encounter black people within Ireland. Often those experiences have been highly

Olaudah Equiano

positive; for example, black campaigners against slavery visited Ireland, people like Olaudah Equiano in the 1790s and Frederick Douglass in the 1840s. Both were delighted at the reception they received, Douglass in particular remarking on the absence of racism. On the other hand, many other black people had arrived in Ireland in much more subordinate positions – whether as Viking slaves in the 9th century or servants, domestics and prostitutes in the 18th. Popular culture played its part in the aetiology of racist attitudes; black and blackface entertainers in the 19th century portrayed black people as objects of humour or pathos, influencing countless Irish people who had never met black people in person to internalise these stereotypes. And also in the 19th century, freak shows brought to Irish audiences such people as the unfortunate Saartjie Baartman, the so-called 'Hottentot Venus', her disability a source of voyeuristic entertainment.

On a few occasions the power relations were reversed. Thus black soldiers, especially drummers and musicians, have accompanied British regiments as they fought battles against the Irish or attempted to pacify the civilian population. Neither experience was guaranteed to have the native Irish think highly of people of colour.

Irish encounters with black people were not confined to Ireland, however. Although itself colonised and thereby unable to boast an empire of its own, Ireland has provided soldiers, sailors and administrators who played a key role in the growth and maintenance of the British Empire. As such, Irish men joined Irish regiments in the British army, fought the Zulus in southern Africa, and policed Bengali revolutionaries in India. In their letters home or when they returned in person, they were able to articulate their imperialist and often racist beliefs for countless other Irish people to hear. Nor were these the first such encounters between black and Irish. Because of restrictive British laws preventing the development of the Irish economy in the 17th and 18th centuries, Ireland did not develop its own slave trade to match that of England. However, Irish people were involved in slavery – whether as slave ship captains or crew, planters and overseers in the West Indies, or soldiers. Moreover, Irish merchants were centrally involved in the provisioning of the slave plantations, to the extent that it could be argued that the economic take-off of, for example, Belfast was no less dependent on slavery than that of Bristol or Liverpool.

Throughout the centuries, the Irish have travelled across the globe – medieval missionaries, Scotch-Irish in the Appalachians, impoverished post-Famine Catholics, emigrants to England, America and Australia, 'wild geese' in the armies of Europe, and officers and rank-and-file soldiers throughout the British Empire, Catholic missionaries in the 19th and 20th centuries. Encounters with people of colour are as ancient as Irish emigration itself. In these situations often the power relations were such that the people of colour were subordinate. In other cases, blacks and Irish emigrants were equally marginalised; such is the case in relation to early Scotch-Irish and Irish Catholic emigrants to America and of convicts to Australia. Sometimes the Irish showed tremendous solidarity with their black neighbours, helping slaves to rebel in the Caribbean or escape in the antebellum southern states of the US. But they also displayed the most racist of attitudes and behaviour, whether it was the Scotch-Irish eagerness to own slaves to prove their own emerging respectability, the anti-black riots of the Catholic Irish in New York and elsewhere as they successfully removed black competition for low-skilled jobs, or the enthusiasm with which newly-freed Irish convicts in Australia engaged in genocide against the Aboriginals.

There is, in short, an ambivalent legacy which emerges. There are of course impressive examples of symmetrical solidarity, with colonised Irish and blacks recognising and embracing each other's struggles for emancipation. For example, the Fenians at one point considered sending arms and instructors to the Zulus to help them engage the British army in southern Africa. Around the same time, recently emancipated slaves in California telegrammed the Fenians offering 40,000 armed black soldiers to fight for Irish freedom – once they have firmly established their own, that is. Yet there is also a great imbalance apparent; for every Daniel O'Connell who railed against American slavery and refused to accept the financial support of slaveholders, there were numerous Marcus Garveys who saw the freedom of Ireland as practically on a par with black liberation. Moreover, the history of black liberation struggle throws up no equivalent of John Mitchel – at the forefront of the struggle for liberation at home while supporting slavery elsewhere.

Our purpose here is not to make cheap revisionist jibes at the expense of the canon of Irish history. Rather it is to expose, albeit briefly, an aspect of Irish history that has been confined to the footnotes of the history books, if considered at all. There are countless accounts of the phenomenon of Irish emigration and the anti-Irish racism experienced by those emigrants (Curtis, 1984; Hickman and Walter, 1997; McVeigh, 1996). There are comprehensive accounts of the anti-semitism in Ireland (Hyman, 1972; Keogh, 1998). There is a growing awareness that the treatment of the Traveller community is an indigenous form of Irish racism (MacLaughlin, 1995; McVeigh, 1992). But there are remarkably few historical accounts which focus specifically on the complex and ambivalent legacy of encounters between Irish people and people of colour both inside and outside Ireland. Within that ambivalence lie the roots of contemporary international solidarity in Ireland as well as the roots of racism. And to begin to uncover the complexity of the history of those encounters is to shed light on the task at hand for those who wish to combat racism in Ireland.[2]

2. Ireland and the Slave Trade

For and against slavery

In the British House of Commons in 1831, during a debate on colonial slavery, the Irish MP Daniel O'Connell spoke passionately for abolition. He vowed to return to Ireland to continue his campaign for abolition, and reminded his fellow MPs that Ireland 'has its glory, that no slave ship was ever launched from any of its numerous ports' (Reid, 1999: 343). O'Connell's opposition to slavery was beyond question. Despite otherwise conventional beliefs, such as his unswerving allegiance to the British monarchy, he stood out as a principled abolitionist. Pursuing Irish-American support for his big political campaigns – Catholic Emancipation, and the Repeal of the Act of Union – he exasperated many by his outspoken condemnation of slave-owning in the southern United States. He rejected the financial support of southern slave-owners: 'I want no American aid if it comes across the Atlantic stained in Negro blood', he stated in 1845 (cited in O'Farrell, 1991: 36).

John Mitchel was a contemporary of O'Connell. As a leading member of the Young Irelanders, he was diametrically opposed to O'Connell on many issues, including that of the use of political violence. Transported to Tasmania for his part in an armed insurrection in Ireland in 1848, Mitchel escaped and went to live in the United States. In 1857, now living in Tennessee, he wrote in the paper he had founded, the *Southern Citizen*:

> I consider Negro slavery here the best state of existence
> for the Negro and the best for his master; and I consider
> that taking Negroes out of their brutal slavery in Africa
> and promoting them to a human and reasonable slavery
> here is good. (MacCall, 1938: 337)

Mitchel was eventually jailed for his outspoken support for the Confederacy.

O'Connell and Mitchel represent a stark contrast in early and mid-19th century Ireland on the issue of slavery. Nor did they stand alone. Abolitionism was well-organised in cities like Belfast, Cork and Dublin, and black people who came to speak at meetings and rallies were impressed by their reception. In contrast, there were many supporters of slavery, some of whom did not confine their support to words. Two ships from Dublin, the *Sylva* and the *Sophia*, were recorded slaving in the Gambia in May 1716. The people being transported to Jamaica on the *Sophia* revolted, killing all of the crew except the captain (Tattersfield, 1998: 349). In July 1718, a Limerick ship, *Prosperity*, is recorded as having transported 96 slaves from Africa to Barbados (*ibid*). And in 1784 Limerick became the first Irish port to publicise the attempt to promote a slave trade company (Rodgers, 2000: 177).

Nevertheless, as Tattersfield (1998: 349) concludes, 'it is doubtful whether this clandestine trade was ever very substantial...' Of much more substance in Irish terms was the involvement of Irish merchants in provisioning the West Indian plantations. Truxes (1988: 5) states, 'the rapid growth of Ireland's provisioning capacity, largely fed by demand from the Caribbean, was one of the chief stimulants to the development of her principal seaports and market towns'. Not only the large towns, but also Derry, Newry, Drogheda and Waterford[3] were intimately tied into the provisioning business. In effect, even though slavery may not have been established in Irish ports as it was in Liverpool and Bristol, Irish merchants were as dependent on slavery as their colleagues in England. O'Connell's claim that 'no slave ship was ever launched' from Irish ports represents a noble aspiration, but it is not correct. There was a darker side to Irish history. Nowhere was that more apparent than in Belfast.

Yet, to first appearances, Belfast in this period was an enlightened town, welcoming to black abolitionists like Olaudah Equiano (see page 3). Equiano was born in Nigeria. He had been enslaved, but later bought his freedom and became a vocal abolitionist. He wrote his life story – *The Interesting Narrative of the Life of Olaudah Equiano or Gustavus Vassa* – and toured widely selling the book and promoting its abolitionist message. He was in Ireland for eight and a half months in 1791. He sold 1900 copies of his book and recorded that he was 'exceedingly well treated, by persons of all ranks'; he 'found the people extremely hospitable, particularly in Belfast' (quoted in Fryer, 1984: 110). In May 1791, he was invited to Belfast by the abolitionist Thomas Digges and by Samuel Neilsen, one of the leading members of the radical republican movement, the Society of United Irishmen. A draper and editor of the movement's paper, the *Northern Star*, Neilsen was noted for being among the most radical of that radical movement. His active support for the abolition of slavery was evident on many occasions. He was not, however, unique. As befitted a movement inspired by the ideals of the French and American revolutions, the United Irishmen broadly supported the abolition of slavery. The metaphor of slavery was used widely in late 18th century Ireland not only to depict the boureoisie's condition, politically and economically hobbled by Britain, but also in relation to the condition of Catholics; thus Henry Grattan, leader of the Patriot Parliament, stated that 'The Irish Protestant can never be free until the Irish Catholic has ceased to be a slave' (Davis, 1975: 368). More than that, the foremost among them, such as Theobald Wolfe Tone, believed that the commitment to the Enlightenment ideal of 'the rights of man' meant the diffusion of those rights to all, including Catholics and black slaves. Others in the United Irishmen in Belfast were merchants who were benefiting directly from the provisioning of the West Indian plantations – such as leading industrialist and linen producer William Sinclair, a founder member of the movement (Rodgers, 1997: 84) – and were perhaps accordingly less vocal on abolition than Tone.

Belfast, trade and slavery

The first merchants in Belfast were English settlers who came around 1611. But by the 1670s Belfast's merchant community was overwhelmingly Scottish. As early as 1665, one of these Scottish merchants, George MacCartney, Sovereign (or Lord Mayor) of Belfast, was exporting beef to Cadiz, Tangiers, La Rochelle and Barbados (Agnew, 1996: 105). His relative, Black George MacCartney, was at the same time exporting fish to Bristol, France and Barbados (*ibid*: 106). Thus, at a relatively early stage in the West Indian plantations, Belfast merchants were already involved in trade.

At that stage, the main crop grown in the West Indies was tobacco. It proved much less suitable a crop in the Caribbean climate than in continental America. Around 1650, beginning in Barbados and eventually subsuming the rest of the islands, the switch was made to sugar production. In a relatively short time, West Indian agriculture became monoculture (Dunn, 1972: 19-20). A labour-intensive exercise, sugar production required more slaves and indentured servants. Initially many of the indentured servants were Irish, persuaded to emigrate because the passage was paid and because, at the end of a set period of work on the plantation, they were promised release from service and a piece of land. Prisoners – again many of them Irish – were also transported and there was also a lucrative trade in kidnapping. In fact, in the 17th century, people seized from Irish, Scottish and English ports and shipped off to the plantations were deemed to have been 'barbadoised' (rather than 'shanghaied', a later development). Although the life facing these people and the indentured servants was rough, some of the Irish sent to the Caribbean were even worse off. Oliver Cromwell sent his son Henry to Ireland with instructions to round up young people as young as 12 and transport them as slaves (O'Callaghan, 2000: 111-121).[4]

Although the initial problem of labour for the sugar plantations was thus solved, the concentration on sugar production created other problems. For example, it tied up the land completely in the production of a single cash crop, leaving the islands' inhabitants almost totally dependent on imported provisions. The early involvement of Belfast merchants in trade with the West Indies ensured that they were well-placed to take advantage of that dependency and at the same time seek an escape from their own dependency on Britain.

A political priority in 18th century Britain was 'that the political status of Ireland should be reduced from that of a kingdom to that of a colony' (O'Brien, 1919: 223). Thus, the royal instructions to Lord Robartes, Viceroy of Ireland were as follows: 'You shall in all things endeavour to advance and improve that trade of that our kingdom [Ireland] so far as it shall not be a prejudice to this our kingdom of England' (cited in Truxes, 1988: 8). The Navigation Acts of 1663, 1670, 1685 and 1696 were central to that goal. They sought to establish an English monopoly on trade with the Caribbean, and thus required the use of English ships and crews in such trade, as well as the loading and unloading of cargo in English ports. Similarly, the Cattle Act of 1663 prohibited the export of Irish cattle to Britain. These acts were clearly – and deliberately – an attempt by England to hinder the economic development of Ireland, as O'Brien (1919: 225) explains:

> ... the two countries had reached almost the same state of industrial development, and both produced the same commodities for export. It was one thing to prohibit the exportation of worked-up commodities from America, where practically no manufactures existed; another to

prohibit their exportation from Ireland, where industrial activity was beginning to develop.

To first appearances, the Navigation and Cattle Acts would seem to have spelt the death knell of the Irish merchant class and indeed Irish ports and merchants did suffer to some extent. For example, up until 1780, Irish linen had to be officially shipped to the Caribbean through English ports. But in fact, the Acts were difficult to enforce; smuggling became part of the Irish merchants' stock in trade. In addition, the application of the Acts, no matter how weakly, encouraged Irish merchants to seek alternative markets in continental Europe and Scandinavia. Finally, there was a loophole in the Navigation Acts which meant that, fortuitously, the provisioning of English ships in Ireland was excluded. As a result, Irish merchants quickly came to dominate trade with the British West Indies.

> Ireland, c. 1680, was the source of over half the food imported into the British West Indies, while the much-better-known trade from the American mainland supplied only one-third. Over the next fifty years the share of the mainland increased, but as late as the 1730s … imports from Ireland into the British and foreign West Indies were still well ahead of those from the mainland (Nash, 1985: 352).

The Navigation and Cattle Acts had not worked as planned. In fact, they backfired. As a result of their diversification, 'Irish agriculture and its associated provisioning industries benefited more directly from demands in the islands than did their counterparts in England' (Truxes, 1988: 4). A wide range of products was exported to the Caribbean, and there were regional variations in the trade. 'From the third quarter of the seventeenth century … the West Indian sugar islands found their principal source of salted beef and butter in the agricultural surplus of Ireland' (*ibid*: 1). Also exported were pork, herrings, bread, cheese, beer, candles and 'large quantities of low-priced linens to the islands to clothe the black slave population' (*ibid*: 4). Galway was the first Irish town to take advantage of supplying the plantations on a large scale, but by the turn of the 18th century it was overtaken by Dublin, Cork and Belfast. Dublin tended to specialise in the traffic of convicts and indentured servants, while for Cork, the main export was beef; in fact, Irish beef was the largest single West Indian import until well into the 18th century (*ibid*: 16). Belfast's exports were linen, wheat, flour and salted fish. In the three years ending December 1775, one quarter of all the vessels entering Bridgetown in Barbados with Irish provisions were from Belfast or Belfast and Cork (*ibid*: 80).

In each of these Irish towns specific merchants began to dominate the West Indian trade. Many had paid employees and agents – often their own relations or in-laws – on the islands with which they traded and some had plantations themselves. There is, however, as noted earlier, only slight evidence of their involvement in the direct trade in slaves from West Africa to the Caribbean. Some – such as the firm of Kennedy, Mulherne and Co., based in Montserrat – are recorded as having been involved in shipping slaves between the islands of the Caribbean (*ibid*: 101).

Belfast benefited immensely from supplying the slave plantations, not least in relation to the sale of agricultural products. But the benefits were not confined to agriculture. The two-way trade with the Caribbean and North America was the stimulus to many developments in craft work and manufacturing. The importation of sugar laid the base for a sugar refining industry. And exporting to the West Indies encouraged such industries as rope making, meat packing, flour milling and the salting of beef and fish. Even shoemaking received a boost. As Rodgers (1997: 83) points out, there were 224 shoemakers in Belfast in 1783 and 312 eight years later. The increase was explained mainly by the concerted attempt to supply the West Indian market, Belfast shoemakers producing broader than usual shoes to fit the slaves' feet. But it was in linen production that Belfast's benefits were most apparent. As the slave population in the Caribbean grew and the white population stabilised, there was a relative decline in the demand for beef, pork and butter and a rise in the demand for low-priced linen and salted herrings (Truxes, 1988: 97). The former products were for the consumption of plantation owners and managers, the latter for the black slaves.[5]

It is not too far-fetched to conclude that the industrial take-off of the north-east of Ireland was built firmly on slavery. Suppliers and manufacturers became rich on the trade. With their wealth, they bought land (and often respectability for those marginal to the Anglican Ascendancy), established banks, and diversified into other manufacturing. As Rodgers (1997: 83) concludes, 'Caribbean connections played a key role in promoting the growth of the town and in launching it upon the course that would transform it into a city'.

Waddell Cunningham

Perhaps the most successful businessman of the latter half of the 18th century was Waddell Cunningham (Truxes, 1988: 114-5: Rodgers, 1997: 80; Chambers, 1983: 35-48; see page 15). He was born in Killead, County Antrim in 1730. At an early age, he emigrated to New York and became involved in trade. He quickly established himself and by 1755 was involved in legitimate business, such as exporting wood from Honduras, as well as the illegitimate business of smuggling. His ships also carried slaves between the islands of the Caribbean. His connections with Belfast had not been severed, and he was soon in partnership with Thomas Greg of Belfast, his future brother-in-law, in the New York-based firm of Greg, Cunningham and Co. Their business ethics seemed flexible; they had few qualms about privateering actions against Spanish and French ships during the Seven Years War; they owned at least four armed vessels. At the same time, the company was also trading illegally with the French in the West Indies, supplying weapons and ammunition among other items. In 1775, the firm was one of the largest shipping companies in New York.

At the end of the Seven Years War Britain took over the Windward Islands – Dominica, Grenada, the Grenadines, St Vincent and Tobago – and Waddell Cunningham acquired a plantation on Dominica, which he called 'Belfast'.

In 1765, Cunningham returned to Belfast, Ireland. As in New York, he quickly established himself in various endeavours. Along with brother-in-law, Thomas Greg, he established a

Waddell
Cunningham

factory for the manufacture of sulphuric acid in Lisburn, as well as continuing to build up his Belfast-based trading empire. He owned his own ships and imported 'rum from Antigua, herrings from Sweden, hemp from St Petersburg, timber from Menel, brandy from France, almonds from Jordan, gin from Holland' (Chambers, 1983: 38) and chemicals for bleaching from Danzig, Spain and America. He was also involved, illegally, in shipping linen for uniforms to the American forces during the War of Independence. He established a sugar refining business, had flour-milling interests, set up a scheme for breeding pack horses and mules for export to the sugar-cane plantations, developed new techniques for salting Donegal herring for export, started a bank, was involved in insurance, and still had time for smuggling tobacco. He also became a landlord. With Thomas Greg he bought the leasehold of several hundred acres of land near Templepatrick, County Antrim from Lord Donegall.[6]

Cunningham was as much at the centre of politics in Belfast as economics. He was in command of the Belfast Volunteers and as such was one of the delegates at the Dungannon Convention in February 1782 which sought to map out a programme for greater economic and political independence for Ireland's bourgeoisie. He was the founding president of Belfast Chamber of Commerce, as well as the first president of the Harbour Board. However, as a Presbyterian, he was blocked from holding political office. So in 1784 Cunningham stood for election as MP in nearby Carrickfergus and soundly defeated the establishment candidate. The defeated candidate, however, managed to unseat the new MP on the charge of corruption on account of the efforts made by Cunningham's Belfast business associates to influence the voters of Carrickfergus. A fresh election was held in March 1785 and Cunningham was narrowly defeated.

As regards political reform, he was a gradualist and frequently crossed swords with the radical United Irishmen on that account. One such cause of dissension was Catholic emancipation. The foremost enlightened thinkers in the United Irishmen accepted the arguments of Wolfe Tone that 'the rights of man' should be conferred immediately on their Catholic fellow citizens. Cunningham was not so eager. When Tone was in Belfast for the formation of the United Irishmen in October 1791, he had dinner at the home of Samuel and Martha McTier; another guest was Waddell Cunningham. Tone noted in his journal that he and Cunningham had 'a furious battle, which lasted two hours, on the Catholic question' (quoted in Chambers 1983: 45). The following year, Tone was again in Belfast for a meeting of

Volunteer delegates. He records in his journal that at 1 am on 13 July 1792, he was awakened from his sleep by Samuel Neilsen (the man who had brought Olaudah Equiano to Belfast the previous year). Neilsen was furious at Waddell Cunningham's behaviour, so he and Tone went to Cunningham's room where they found 'delegates from the country corp, with Waddell haranguing against the Catholics'. Tone concludes by giving his opinion of Cunningham: 'Waddell a lying old scoundrel' (Bartlett, 1998: 133).

Nor was Cunningham any more progressive on that other issue dear to the hearts of United Irishmen like Neilsen and Tone, the abolition of black slavery. One of the effects of the Navigation Acts had been to prevent the emergence of an official slaving industry in Ireland. But in 1780, the Acts were fully repealed. In 1786, Cunningham called a meeting with a view to establishing a slave-trading company in Belfast. Also at the meeting was a radical, later member of the United Irishmen, Thomas McCabe. A jeweller with a shop in Smithfield, he was referred to by Tone and Neilsen as 'the slave' after having hung a sign saying 'An Irish Slave' outside his shop in protest at raids by British soldiers. The United Irishman Dr William Drennan, in a letter to his sister Martha McTier, recounted what happened at the meeting.

> I had a letter lately from T[homas] McCabe to tell me of an association planned by Waddell Cunningham for carrying on the slave trade at Belfast to which he had got several subscribers, but which Tom had knocked up completely by writing in the proposal book: 'May G__ eternally damn the soul of the man who subscribes the first guinea'. I could not but smile at receiving this letter and anecdote in Mrs C's presence (letter of 17 May 1806; Agnew, 1999: 480).

This incident has been at the centre of much debate since. Thomas McCabe's son Bernard told the story to Dr R.R. Madden who included it in his 1846 edition of *The United Irishmen: Their Lives and Times*. Subsequently the story was reproduced in

Robert Young's *Old Belfast*, published in 1895, and embellished with an illustration by local artist J.W. Carey (see page 20). Finally, in 1926, S. Shannon Millin set out 'to free the name of Waddell Cunningham from the charge of promoting a slave trade company' (Millin, 1926: 29). He argued that as the story was first told in 1846, 60 years after the incident allegedly occurred, and the linking of Waddell Cunningham directly to the incident was not made until a further 50 years later, it was undoubtedly apocryphal. However, the letter of Dr Drennan to his sister is a much more contemporaneous piece of evidence and one not mentioned by Millin. In the light of that evidence, it would seem that Waddell Cunningham was being true to form; the man who owned a plantation in Dominica until his dying day and whose fortune was built on servicing the system of slavery was at the forefront of the active supporters of that system in Belfast.

Cunningham was a key representative of that section of the Presbyterian bourgeoisie whose self-interest inspired them to oppose the British government on behalf of the greater economic and political freedom for their class, but did not extend to support for the emancipation of Catholics or the abolition of slavery. Tone and Neilsen represented another section of that class, those whose commitment – even to the point of armed insurrection – to the ideals of the Enlightenment led them to argue for political freedom not only for their class, but also for those much less advantaged than themselves, Catholics and slaves.

Abolition

This was the ambivalent atmosphere which Olaudah Equiano encountered in his happy but brief visit to Belfast in 1791. He returned to England where the debate on the abolition of slavery was heating up.

Two decades before Equiano arrived in Ireland, Lord Mansfield, the Chief Justice of England, delivered a judgement which was widely misinterpreted at the time as being much more liberal than it actually was (Fryer, 1984: 20-26). A black slave,

James Somerset, had run away from his American master in England but was recaptured. The abolitionist Granville Sharp, committed to using the courts to challenge the legality of slavery, learned that Somerset was to be shipped back to America. Sharp applied to the High Court for a writ of habeas corpus, which was granted. The abolitionist case was that a slave was free by virtue of setting foot on English soil, no matter what law pertained locally in the colonies; Somerset could therefore not be forced to return to America. In July 1772, Lord Mansfield agreed. In fact, his judgement was a narrow and cautious one, stating merely that a master could not force a slave to travel out of England. However, it was taken by many, at the time and since, as in effect legally abolishing slavery in England. It was 1807 before an Act outlawed slave trading by British subjects, and 1834 before the final emancipation of slaves in Britain and the colonies came about. But in that period, confusion about the law prevailed, not just in England, but also in Ireland. Early in 1833, a slave ship arrived in Waterford from the Azores. An African slave, with a few words of English, came off the ship and was told by some local people that, as a result of setting foot on United Kingdom soil (as a result of the Act of Union of 1801), he was free. The slave was reported to have danced with delight. He was then treated to a drink by a local chimney sweep, after which the two went to the mayor's office. The mayor confirmed that the slave was now free and 'the black and the Irish chimney sweep then left the office arm in arm' (Drescher, 1986: 46). The ship's captain forfeited a $300 surety as a result of failing to deliver the slave to the American who had bought him.

Cunningham's 1786 meeting held to form a slave-trading company in Belfast, as illustrated by J.W.Carey in 1895 (pages 17-18).

3. Precursors

Early contacts

The unexpected visit of this unnamed African to Ireland was not the first encounter between the Irish and people of colour. Although an island off the edge of continental Europe, Ireland was never totally isolated. Trade, warfare and religion ensured that foreigners came to the island and the island's inhabitants travelled abroad. Inuit harpoon-heads dating from between the 10th and 13th centuries have been found in County Down (Forbes, 1988: 13). There is evidence of trade with the Mediterranean area one and a half millennia before the Christian era. It is likely that Phoenician merchants, who are known to have traded with Cornwall, also reached Ireland. And

> glass beads of Egyptian or Aegean origin have been found in eight sites here, while Mycenaean bronze double axes (from about the 12th century B.C.) have been excavated in two places in Ireland. Similarly, it has been claimed that porcellanite axe-heads from Tievebulliagh, Co. Antrim have been recorded in the Eastern Mediterranean (Costelloe, 1974: 3).[7]

Given such contacts, it is entirely possible that the Irish encountered black sailors or merchants long before the Christian era.

Christianity from the fifth century onwards brought new opportunities for contact. In the west of Ireland in particular early monasteries were 'eremitical, deriving their inspiration from the Syrian and Egyptian ascetics' of the early church (Weir, 1980: 59). Later, the proliferation of independent monasteries was in marked contrast to the centralised church which developed under Roman influence. As Roman civilisation succumbed to barbarian influxes and the 'dark ages' emerged, Irish monasticism

> experienced an influx of anchorites and monks fleeing before the barbarian hordes... 'All the learned men on this side of the sea,' claims a note in a Leyden manuscript of this time, 'took flight for transmarine places like Ireland, bringing about a great increase of learning ... to the inhabitants of those regions.' But not a few of these men were bone-thin ascetics from such Roman hinterlands as Armenia, Syria, and the Egyptian desert. The Ulster monastery of Bangor, for instance, claimed in its litany to be 'ex Aegypto transducta' ('translated from Egypt'); and the convention of using red dots to adorn manuscript initials, a convention that soon became a mark of Irish manuscripts, had first been glimpsed by the Irish in books that the fleeing Copts brought with them (Cahill, 1995: 180).

The Litanies of the early Irish church make it clear that monks from throughout Europe and North Africa came to Ireland. Cerrui, the bishop of Killeigh, Co. Offaly in the 9th century, was Armenian. And according to the 8th century *Litany of Aengus*, seven Coptic monks are buried in one place (Costelloe, 1974: 13-14).[8]

Irish monks began to travel abroad on missionary work from the 6th century onwards, eventually bringing the Christian religion to Scotland, northern England, France, Germany, Switzerland and Italy. In doing so, they 'saved civilization' (Cahill, 1995). As libraries declined throughout the 'dark ages' and literacy became virtually non-existent, it was left to the wandering Irish monks to copy and disseminate the classics of

Greek and Roman, and to some extent Hebrew, literature. In addition, 'illiterate Europe would hardly have developed its great national literatures without the example of Irish, the first vernacular literature to be written down' (*ibid*: 193).

The Vikings

By this point, the Vikings were showing a distinct interest in Ireland. The popular historical view is of a vibrant Gaelic order and flowering monasticism threatened and almost destroyed by hordes of marauding Norsemen. The current, more sober historical assessment is that the effect of the Vikings on the decline of the old tribal, family-based Gaelic order was much less stark than traditionally believed. That order was already in decline prior to the Viking raids. Similarly, Irish monasticism's problems cannot be laid solely at the feet of the Vikings. For example, many monasteries built round towers, high stone structures with doors ten feet or more from the ground. The popular view is that they were built as virtually impregnable structures in the face of Viking attacks. While they were undoubtedly used for protection from the Vikings, their erection pre-dates these attacks. Many monasteries were attacked and destroyed by monks and supporters from other monasteries.

The Viking hit-and-run attacks began in 795. But in 841, Viking influence in Ireland entered a new phase with the establishment of two permanent settlements – one in Annagassan, near Dundalk, the other in Dublin (Clarke, 1990: 92-3). Viking settlement in Ireland was in fact much less limited than in England and Scotland and probably therefore less devastating to the existing order. And like many later invaders, the Vikings seem to have become fairly quickly incorporated into the local Irish scene; by the late 9th century, they were 'just another factor in the tangled web of native Irish political alliances' (Ó Cróinin, 1995: 240). But they constituted an important factor nonetheless. 'By the end of the ninth century, and again during the tenth century, the Kingdom of Dublin –

called by the Norse Dyflinnarskiri – had become one of the most important in Western Europe' (*ibid*: 244). Dublin was a large settlement, certainly by Irish standards, a town (in a society which had few towns), a market and an important port. As a port, it gave the Vikings a permanent base, except in the period 902-917, to plunder far and wide (Clarke 1990: 94). Part of that plunder involved the slave trade.

Slaves had existed in Gaelic Ireland before the Vikings, where they were regarded as a luxury item and as such could be given as tributes or gifts.[9] What the Vikings added was a sophisticated system of slave-trading, with Dublin as the centre of an international market. Slaves were captured in raids in Scotland and England and around 1000 AD were being shipped to markets in Rouen (Doherty, 1980: 84), Iceland, Scandinavia and possibly Arabic Spain (Sheehan, 1998: 175). The Irish were introduced to this venture by the Vikings and soon joint slaving raids were commonplace (Sheehan, 1998: 175; Doherty, 1980: 71).

Much of the information on this period comes from various Irish Annals which list records of occurrences year by year, but also contain longer entries or chronicles, stories and poems. It is likely that all the Annals currently extant derive ultimately from one single text, compiled under the O'Neills in the early 10th century (Radner, 1978: xiii). Because of the Annals, there is a wealth of information available about Ireland prior to 1200 AD. The names of around 30,000 historical persons are known in the Irish case, compared to only a few hundred Anglo-Saxons of the same period and even fewer people from the Germanic kingdoms (Ó Cróinin, 1995: 63). The Annals were compiled by perhaps the most powerful clan in Ireland as proof of their previous greatness now under pressure from various influences, including centralised Christendom. Moreover, some of the stories – while not in the same genre as the clearly mythical tales of, for example, the Fenian Cycle – are embellished. Despite these shortcomings, the Annals provide a remarkable window, even if somewhat clouded, on the times.

There is one source known as the *Fragmentary Annals of Ireland*. Its origins are possibly in the *Leabhar Cluana Eidnech* from the 11th or 12th century. It was transcribed by Giolla Mac Aedhagáin, probably at the beginning of the 15th century, and that copy was itself transcribed in 1643 by Dubhaltach Mac Fir Bhisigh. Although both transcriptions have been lost, a partial transcription was discovered in Brussels. The fragment is regarded as authentic and reliable; it 'adds quite a bit to our knowledge of the Viking period ... The entire chronicle seems to have been assembled during the Viking period' (Radner, 1978: xxv).

The *Fragmentary Annals* record one event for the year 867. Two younger sons of Albdan, king of Norway, drove out the eldest son, Ragnall, in a dispute over the kingship. Ragnall settled in the Orkneys, from whence his sons went to war against the Franks and Saxons. They eventually reached Spain, destroying and plundering, and then crossed the straits to 'Mauretania' in Africa.

> ...the Norwegians swept across the country, and they devastated and burned the whole land. Then they brought a great host of them captive with them to Ireland, ie those are the black men ... Now the black men remained in Ireland for a long time (Radner, 1978: 121).

How were these black slaves received in Ireland? What did it do to Irish culture to see that the only black people they had encountered had come as slaves? The Annals cannot help in this regard.

Three centuries of Viking involvement in Ireland left a legacy in the Gaelic language. Many nautical terms – like 'bád' for 'boat' (Old Norse being 'bátr') – and words to do with aspects of urban living – such as 'sráid' for 'street' (Old Norse 'straeti') – come straight from the Viking language (Ó Cróinin, 1995: 70). In Old Norse, black men were referred to as 'blamadr', literally 'blue men'. In similar vein, it is noteworthy that the antiquity of early encounters between the Irish and people of colour is betrayed by the fact that the Gaelic for 'black man' comes, not from English, but directly from Old Norse: 'fear gorm', or 'blue man' (see also Haliday, 1969: 116).

Ireland and Islam

The Viking raids on North Africa and elsewhere led to the first tentative contacts between Ireland and the Muslim world. Following Viking raids on Andulusia in the early 9th century, an attempt was made to establish a truce. The Vikings sent envoys to the Muslim emir Abd al-Rahman II of Cordova, who in return sent an embassy to the Vikings. The Muslim ambassador, Yahya ibn al-Hakam al-Bakri, visited a Viking court in either Ireland or Denmark, probably in 845 (Lewis 1982: 93).[10] One hundred years later, Ibrahim ibn Yaqub al-Israili al-Turtushi left the same court and travelled in France, Holland, Germany, Bohemia, Poland and Italy. His writings became the basis for Muslim views of a large part of Europe for years to come. Thus, when in the early 11th century one of the greatest Muslim geographers, Ibn al-Faqih, wrote of Ireland he was able to note that 'the Vikings have no firmer base than this island in the whole world' (ibid: 144). He also provided what seems to be a fairly accurate account of Irish methods of whaling at the time, even though neither he nor Ibrahim ibn Yaqub had visited Ireland. Scant as their knowledge is, it is significant. Classical western scholars, on whom Muslim scholars also drew, do not mention a Viking presence in Ireland at this point. Jones' (1978: 8) explanation is that the Muslim knowledge derives from contacts through Viking raids on Muslim territory, especially in Spain.

The high point of Muslim geographical scholarship in the period is the *Book of Roger*, or *Nuzhat al-Mushtaq*, commissioned by Roger II, the Norman king of Sicily, and compiled by Abu Abdallah Muhammad al-Sherif al-Idrisi in the early 10th century. He writes of a remote place, Ireland, and gives an account of a war between the inhabitants which led to the ruin of the three cities on the island (Lewis 1982: 148).

According to James (1978: 6-7), this is likely to be a reference to 'the wars between Munster, Leinster and Connacht, culminating in the burning of Limerick in 1063'.

The Crusades

Scant as Muslim knowledge of Ireland in the period seems to have been, there is even less evidence of Irish knowledge of the Muslim world. Viking raids apart, the other main point of contact would seem to have been as a result of pilgrimage to the Holy Land. According to the 8th century *Litany of Aengus*, such pilgrimages were common among both clergy and laity. The *Book of Leinster* notes that St Brendan was among many Irish monks who made the pilgrimage (Costelloe, 1974: 23). From 1010, that journey became more difficult with the capture of the Holy Land by the Seljurian Turks. By 1070, the Saracens were in control and pilgrimage became impossible. Then in 1095, Pope Urban II called for a crusade to free the holy places. Over the next 200 years three major Crusades occurred. Mobilisation for these Crusades took place all over Christendom, including Ireland. Irish nobles, bishops and monks journeyed to 'the stream' (the River Jordan). Members of the De Burgh family were probably on the First Crusade and with the arrival of the Normans in Ireland in 1169, there were numerous other links to crusading. The knights whose names are known were from Norman or Norman-Irish ruling families. They brought with them on their Crusades servants and retainers who must have appeared as anachronistic to the well-armed knights of continental Europe. One 11th century chronicler, Guibert of Nogent, notes of the First Crusade: 'From the distant bogs and mountains of Ireland issued some naked and savage fanatics, ferocious at home, but unwarlike abroad' (cited in Costelloe, 1974: 28).

The Normans were conquerors in Ireland and took some time before they became 'more Irish than the Irish themselves'. This may well have coloured popular views in Ireland regarding the

Crusades. For example, the Knights Templar and Knights Hospitaller had arrived in Ireland with King Henry II and Strongbow, were given large tracts of land confiscated from the Irish, and became a loyal and efficient garrison force; 'neither seem to have had the slightest sympathy with the native Irish' (Costelloe, 1974: 45).

At the same time, the Crusades were preached throughout Ireland and funds – known as 'saladines' – were collected in each diocese for their upkeep. Given that, and the unknown number of native Irish who travelled with their masters, the Crusades undoubtedly impacted on Ireland and left a particular view of Islam. In Spain, the struggle with Islam left many visible cultural signs. Saint James, after whom the great pilgrimage site of Santiago de Compostela was named, was known as Santiago Matamoros – 'Moorslayer' – and that surname remains in the Spanish-speaking world. Matamoros also became a place name, as for example in the Mexican town on the border near Brownsville, Texas. Such signs testify to the intensity of the holy war between Christendom and the Islamic world. There are no such visible signs – surnames[11] and town names – in Ireland. But the widespread view that there were infidels in possession of places holy to Christianity and that they had to be removed by force undoubtedly confirmed specific prejudices about people of colour in early medieval Ireland.

Barbary slaves

That view was often confirmed by later encounters. From the 16th to the early 19th century, pirates – corsairs – from the Arab cities of Algiers, Tripoli and Tunis in North Africa raided both shipping and coastal areas around the Mediterranean for Christian slaves. In the 1580s, it was estimated that more than a quarter of Algiers' population of 100,000 consisted of such 'Barbary slaves' (Clissold, 1977: 53). Often the slaves were put to work, not least as galley slaves in the pirate ships. But they were also seen as a source of profit, not just because of their labour, but also because they could attract large ransoms in return for their freedom.

Conditions for the Barbary slaves were frequently grim, especially in the bagnios, or overcrowded prisons or on the pirate ships. But, there was one way of escape open to most of them – conversion to Islam. Those who relinquished their Christian beliefs – an awesome move given beliefs in eternal damnation – were sometimes genuine, but others did so for opportune reasons. For the benefits of conversion were many. Unlike Muslims held by Christian societies, conversion conferred equal citizenship. Renegade Christians could not be galley slaves, could marry Muslims, if male, could inherit wealth or property from a former master who died intestate, and could hold important political or military office. Thus, more than half of the 23 high officials in Algiers in the 1580s were renegade Europeans and 25 of the 33 captains of pirate ships were renegades or sons of renegades (*ibid*: 87).

One such captain was Morat Rais, formerly known as Jan Janssen, a Dutch adventurer. With improvements in Arab ship design and building, Janssen was able to venture as far abroad as Iceland and Ireland in pursuit of slaves. In 1631, he raided the town of Baltimore in County Cork and carried off hundreds of its inhabitants (*ibid*: 54).[12]

These were not the only Irish to be enslaved in North Africa. In 1747 a group of soldiers from the Hibernian Regiment, serving with Spanish forces in Italy, were captured on their way from Italy to Spain.[13] The group consisted of a Lieutenant Colonel, six captains, ten subalterns and sixty privates, along with some women and children (*ibid*: 152). In Algiers, one of the women, Mrs Jones, was assaulted by a janissary and took refuge in a loft. To force her to come down, the janissary severed the hand of one of her small children, at which point she threw down a broken millstone, breaking the janissary's leg. In retaliation, he killed her child. She then came down and, taking his scimatar, beheaded him (*ibid*: 40-1).

Other Irish captives appear from time to time, including two bishops of Limerick. One, referred to only as Tomás Hibernico, was captured on his return from Rome in 1591. Although freed on ransom, he stayed on to minister to the other slaves (*ibid*: 123). The other, Edmund Dwyer, was taken captive on his way back to Ireland from France in 1644. He was held as a slave in Smyrna until his ransom was paid by the Irish wife of a French merchant in the city (Lenihan, 1967: 591). There was also an Irish gun-founder named Carr who was in charge of the Sultan of Morocco's only cannon foundry in 1727 (Clissold, 1997: 98).

Slaves, servants and soldiers

It was, however, the Christian nations of the west which were eventually to take slavery and turn it into a system which was central to capitalist development. In 1415 the Portuguese captured the Moorish stronghold of Ceuta, thus opening up the way for the European penetration of Africa (Shyllon, 1974: 1-2). By 1435, the Portuguese had reached Senegal and by 1481, the Congo. As early as 1441 Antam Goncalves brought back the first cargo of black slaves to Lisbon.

English adventurers were relatively slow off the mark; it was 1530 before William Hawkins made the first English voyage to West Africa. Twenty five years later, in 1555, John Lok brought back the first African blacks to London, five Ghanaians who were to be educated and returned to Africa as middle men for trade (Fryer, 1984: 5).

In 1493, a papal bull had debarred Spain from any African possessions. As a result, Spain conferred on the merchant fleets of other nations the right to supply black slaves to Spain and its colonies. This was known as the Asiento. In 1600 Portugal received the Asiento, and in 1640 it was transferred to the Dutch. The French acquired the Asiento in 1701 and in 1713 the English hit the jackpot with a contract to supply 144,000 slaves at the rate of 4,800 per year. England now became the great slave trader of the world.

Even before the buying and selling of black people began in England itself, black people were making their way to England as servants, prostitutes and court entertainers (Fryer, 1984: 8). Some also made it through the military route, as soldiers and army drummers. Take the case of Prince William of Orange. He landed at Brixham on 5 November 1688 to claim the English crown from his father-in-law, King James II. He decided to make a flamboyant entry into Exeter four days later.

> First came 300 cavalry, mounted on impressive Flanders horses, followed by 200 of the first Negroes the country people had ever seen, brought over from the Dutch colony in Surinam, colourfully dressed in embroidered capes lined with fur and plumes of white feathers on their heads (Van Der Zee, 1973: 254).

The involvement of King William III, as he became, in Irish affairs is well-known. What is unclear is if any of these black soldiers accompanied his army on his Irish campaign. Ferguson (1990) gives a comprehensive account of the Williamite troops and their commanders at the Battle of the Boyne, but mentions no black soldiers.

That said, it is still possible that there were black faces at the Boyne. William's mother, Mary Stuart, in line with the fashion of the time, had a black body servant and had her portrait painted along with the servant (see page 32). William himself 'had a favourite black slave, a bust of whom used to be on display at Hampton Court, complete with "carved white marble collar, with a padlock, in every respect like a dog's collar"' (Fryer, 1984: 22-3). And Friedrich Herman, 1st Duke of Schomberg and King William's Captain-General who was killed at the Battle of the Boyne, had his portrait painted with a black servant holding his helmet (see page 34). Did the King or his Captain-General bring their black slaves with them to Ireland? There is no historical evidence to say they did, yet it appears a distinct possibility.[14] What the rank and file Williamite soldiers may have thought of such black men is well captured in some lines written at the time by the poet John Dryden. He proposes that English soldiers in Ireland should

> Each bring his Love, a Bogland Captive home,
> Such proper Pages, will long Trayns become;
> With copper-collars, and with brawny Backs,
> Quite to put down the Fashion of our Blacks
> (cited in Fryer, 1984: 23).

How the Irish might have viewed such black visitors cursed with the double stigma of being enslaved and associated with a conquering army is not recorded.

Mary Stuart

The presence of black soldiers in Ireland as part of the British army is documented occasionally. Thus, 'many regiments quartered in Ireland had black drummers; at least one, the 29th Regiment, all black drummers' (Hart: 8). Fryer (1984: 84) also refers to these drummers. There were eight or ten of them in total and they came from Gaudaloupe. The Regiment needed special permission from the king to bring them to Ireland.

On at least one occasion, black soldiers set foot in Ireland as part of a liberating force rather than a conquering or occupying one. French troops under General Humbert landed in Killala, County Mayo in 1798 in support of the United Irishmen's insurrection. They expressed great frustration at their failure to organise the local peasantry into a well-disciplined force. There were a number of reasons for this, one of which related to the origins of some of the French officers.

> The Connaught peasantry were willing enough to take the uniforms and arms which were distributed ... but ... they were not equally ready to respond to the commands of their officers and submit to the coercion of discipline. Untrained and unused to military exercises, they were found unfit to be trusted with the more responsible duties of garrison troops, and the work of sappers to which they were set they deemed beneath their dignity, the more so as among the French officers over them were some men of colour from St. Domingo, to whom they thought it insulting to be subjected (Falkiner, 1902: 299-300).

But not every such encounter was so fraught. Lord Edward Fitzgerald (Tillyard, 1997) was an officer with a British regiment, the 19th Regiment of Foot, in America.[15] At the battle of Eutaw Creek, near Charleston, on 8 September 1781, he was critically injured and left for dead on the battlefield. An African slave named Tony Small, who had escaped as the white population left the area ahead of the battle, discovered Fitzgerald, brought him back to his hut and nursed him back to health. It was the beginning of a relationship which lasted the rest of Lord Edward Fitzgerald's lifetime. Tony travelled with him to

Ireland and later on explorations in Canada. Back in Ireland in 1798, Fitzgerald was now in charge of military planning for the United Irishmen. In March 1798, the British authorities, acting on the basis of information from informers, attempted to round up the leaders of the Society in Dublin. Fitzgerald escaped and went into hiding. However, he was betrayed and fatally wounded resisting arrest. He and Tony Small had been inseparable, to the extent that he had had Small's portrait painted, a unique example in Ireland of a portrait of a black man without his master (for a reproduction, see Crookshank and the Knight of Glin, 1979: 132; also Tillyard 1997). Small made it clear that he did not want to know Fitzgerald's whereabouts when he was in hiding so that the information could not be extracted from him under torture. Edward Fitzgerald died in prison a few days after his arrest without seeing his friend Tony Small again. Small, his wife Julie and son Moiricio, accompanied Fitzgerald's widow Pamela, first to London and then Hamburg. And when Pamela remarried in Hamburg, the Smalls returned to London where Tony died a few years later.

*Friedrich,
Duke of Schomberg*

4. Plantation and Conquest

The Scotch-Irish

In 1607 the leaders of the northern clans in Ireland – in particular, the O'Neills and O'Donnells – defeated in battles with the Elizabethan English armies, left for continental Europe. The event is known as 'the Flight of the Earls' and the fugitives and their descendants as 'the Wild Geese'. It was the final nail in the coffin of the old Gaelic order.

Ulster was now seized by the English and land given to various adventurers and militarists. In their wake, perhaps 100,000 settlers were planted in Ulster on land confiscated from the native Irish in the period up to 1641. The bulk of these settlers – around 70,000 – were English, but there were also 30,000 Scots planters. The attraction to Ireland for the Scots was escape from poverty in Scotland and the chance of making a fortune in a new land. They were determined, tough pioneers, settling on escheated land and subject to the disdain of the natives they had displaced. They were 'the hard men of frontier society' (Ohlmeyer, 1998: 132), and as such were used quite cynically by those higher up the social hierarchy – usually English and Anglican – as a buffer against the 'uncivilised natives'. Hence, a Mr Taylor wrote his 'Proposition for Planting My Lord of Essex's Land' in 1622, in which he foresaw that 'the Scotch shall be as a wall betwixt them [the English] and the Irish through which quarter the Irish will not pass to carry any stealths' (quoted in Canny, 1998: 13). Experiences such as the native uprising of 1641, which almost destroyed the entire plantation endeavour in Ulster, made them even harder men (and women).

Ulster did not turn out to be the promised land they had been led to expect. The rents were high, as Presbyterians, they were second-class citizens, and an even newer land of opportunity beckoned – America. By the end of the 17th century they were emigrating in their thousands; around 250,000 emigrated between 1726 and 1776, and a further 100,000 between then and the end of the 18th century (Jones, 1969: 49), by which point it was estimated that one-sixth of the European population of the new nation was of Scotch-Irish birth or descent (Evans, 1969: 75).

They headed first to New England, but were not accepted there, so from about 1720, most Scotch-Irish emigrants landed in Philadelphia and Delaware. 'No group before the Scotch-Irish had arrived in such complete destitution', says Oakes (1983: 15). They could not afford to settle near Philadelphia – nor would the genteel burghers of that city have happily accepted them. So they 'almost invariably headed for the back country' (*ibid*: 16), where land was cheap or free. But life was also more difficult there, not least because of confrontations with the native Americans. For example, in 1763 they faced the onslaught of Chief Pontiac of the Ottowas who was heading a confederation of Indian nations against the settlers. Fitzpatrick (1989: 80) points out that this, 'unlike the later Indian Wars, was an evenly matched struggle'. That said, the skill and on occasions brutality with which they embarked on the fight with the natives was the cutting edge of the later genocide of the native Americans.[16] Of course, they suffered greatly from native attacks, once again as in Ireland, forming a buffer between the 'uncivilised' natives and the upper-class settlers. James Logan, a Quaker from Lurgan, County Armagh and Colonial Secretary in Pennsylvania was quite strategic on this point; echoing the words of Mr Taylor, also from

Armagh, over a century earlier, he said: 'I thought it might be prudent to plant a Settlement of those who had so bravely defended Derry and Inniskillen as a frontier in case of any Disturbance' (cited in Fitzpatrick, 1989: 73).

Paradoxically, the Scotch-Irish were also the settlers who learned most from the natives. They dressed in buckskins, became as adept as the natives at hunting and tracking, and learned native skills of agriculture and herbal medicine. Once again, they were the hard men of the frontier at the edges of settler society. They also pushed back that frontier. 300,000 of them 'poured through the Cumberland Gap between 1775 and 1800' (Evans, 1969: 75), eventually opening up the Shenandoah Valley of Virginia and the Carolinas to European settlement. Their most famous representatives were not merely frontiersmen like Davy Crockett and Kit Carson and Civil War generals like Ulysses S. Grant and Stonewall Jackson, but also presidents such as Andrew Jackson and Woodrow Wilson, and millionaires such as the Getty and Mellon dynasties.

Thomas Mellon was born in County Tyrone in 1813. In America he became a lawyer, a judge, and a property speculator, and eventually patriarch of one of America's richest families. Clearly he was a man whom white, Anglo-Saxon, Protestant America had no difficulty assimilating; his racist views fitted well with the prejudices of the WASP establishment. As a judge, he was approached on one occasion by a lawyer seeking a charter to build a Jewish cemetery. He replied, 'A place to bury Jews? – with pleasure, with pleasure' (Fitzpatrick, 1989: 154). He despised Irish Catholics too and suggested that a solution to the political problems of Ireland would be to disperse the populaton as widely as possible throughout the world 'where they would disappear like a bad smell in the fresh air of other cultures' (*ibid*: 156).

Of course, not all the poor Scotch-Irish immigrants were as successful as Thomas Mellon. However, they did manage overall to lose their label as outcasts and achieve a level of respectability. As in Mellon's case, a key element in their assimilation was racism. 'The ownership of slaves became for many immigrants the single most important symbol of their success in the New World' (Oakes, 1983: 43). It was also more than a symbol but also a key factor in their upward mobility. Of no group of immigrants was this more true than of the Scotch-Irish. Arriving in America practically destitute, they 'are certain in a few years to acquire money enough to buy a negro, which they are said to be invariably ambitious to possess' (Frederick Law Olmstead, quoted in Oakes, 1983: 42). This was a deep irony: a group of people who had left Ireland to escape poverty became committed to ensuring that other human beings could never own the profits of their own labour; who had resented legal oppression against them by the established church in Ireland could themselves legally oppress others; and who had been among the first to join the Continental Army and to fight resolutely for independence and democracy could later fight to withhold the benefits of that revolution from others. The answer to this paradox is that their actions were not irrational, but were the logical outcome of their intense faith in economic liberalism. They would never be large plantation owners; in fact, they were unlikely to ever own more than one slave at a time and therefore were quite untypical slave owners. But like the Virginia tobacco 'aristocrats', the poor Scotch-Irish farmers 'in the back country ... grew prosperous, albeit more modestly, on the diversified products of slave labor' (*ibid*: 25). They saw themselves as having the same right to prosper as the 'aristocrat' and by the same means, and later many of them defended that right and those means in the Civil War. They believed that if the sine qua non of prosperity for the 'aristocrats' was the right to own slaves, then it was at least as essential for 'poor white trash'. And it was ultimately in that common espousal of economic liberalism with the big slave owners that the Scotch-Irish came in from the margins and became American.

The Catholic Irish

A remarkably similar transformation occurred in the case of a later wave of Irish immigrants to America, the Irish who arrived in droves in the 19th century, especially after the Famine of mid-century. Irish Catholics on the early plantations were 'doubly damned as foreign and papist' (Jordan, 1977: 87). Many of these early Irish migrants were there entirely involuntarily. Rounded up by Oliver Cromwell's son Henry, they were sent as slaves to Barbados where they were treated abominably (O'Callaghan 2000). The situation for those Irish migrants who were technically not slaves, but servants, was often little better. As early as 1654, anti-Irish discrimination was enacted in Virginia law, with Irish servants arriving without indentures having to serve longer than similar English servants (Higginbotham, 1978: 34).[17] In 1698, ship's captains were paid a bounty for each non-Irish, white male servant they imported into South Carolina; they were also required to certify 'that to the best of their knowledge none of the servants by them imported be either what is commonly called native Irish or persons of known scandalous characters or Roman Catholics' (*ibid*: 160). Loyal whites were regarded as being at a premium in terms of defence against native Americans. But as the number of black slaves grew, a fear in many of the colonies was that black slaves and disloyal white servants would collaborate. Thus laws in South Carolina specified that a white servant who ran away in the company of slaves would be declared a felon and was 'to suffer death without the benefit of clergy' (*ibid*: 158).

By the time slavery was established as a widespread institution, black slaves and Irish immigrants were clearly side by side at the bottom of America's social class hierarchy, much to the annoyance of the blacks who referred to the Irish as 'white niggers' and 'considered their presence in Negro neighborhoods undesirable' (Litwack, 1961: 164). Astounding as it may appear, in some respects, Irish labourers in the mid-19th century were worse off than black slaves. The latter represented a financial investment on the part of the planter, while the former were expendable. An injured free labourer was not the potential burden to an employer that a disabled slave could be to the master; hence the willingness of planters to risk the health of their Irish labourers, a fact commented on by numerous travellers in the southern states. Phillips (1966: 246) gives the example of John Burnside, an Irish immigrant himself, who became a major slave owner. He employed Irish labourers for ditching and other severe work so an not to endanger the health of his slaves. A contemporary traveller, M.W. Philips, summed up the logic succinctly: 'Planters must guard their slaves' health and life as among the most vital of their own interests; for while crops were merely income, slaves were capital' (*ibid*: 301).

The inveterate traveller, Frederick Law Olmsted, had many observations on the use of Irish labour. On one occasion he observed a gang of Irish labourers digging ditches and asked the overseer why he was not using slaves for the job. The reply was: 'It's dangerous work, and a negro's life is too valuable to be risked at it. If a negro dies, it's a considerable loss, you know' (Olmsted, 1953: 70). On another occasion, in Alabama, he witnessed slaves and Irish immigrants working together to load bales of cotton onto a ship. The slaves stood at the top of a ramp and rolled the heavy cotton bales down. The Irish stood at the bottom where they were meant to direct the moving bales into a hold. But the bales frequently bounced crazily, breaking railings and injuring anyone in their path. Olmsted sought out the ship's mate, who explained: 'The niggers are worth too much to be risked here; if the Paddies are knocked overboard, or get their backs broke, nobody loses anything' (*ibid*: 215).

Of course, there were limits to the use of Irish labourers. Despite all, as free labourers they still had rights and expectations. Thus Phillips (1966: 337) notes the case of a planter near New Orleans in the 1840s who tried to replace slave labour with Irish and German immigrants. They struck for double pay and he lost around $10,000 worth of crops. In similar vein, Litwack (1980: 353) records the comments of an English traveller in Virginia on attempts to introduce immigrant labour.

> Swedes, Germans and Irishmen had been imported; but the Swedes refused to eat cornbread, the Germans sloped away north-west-ward, in the hope of obtaining homesteads, and the Irishmen preferred a city career. It seems that the south will have need of Sambo yet awhile...

Despite the proximity of slaves and Irish at the bottom of the hierarchy, there were recorded instances of mutual aid. For example, black slaves who escaped to the north not only were frequently helped by other blacks (despite the penalties, including death, threatened), but also: 'some whites, among whom the Irish are most often mentioned, helped fugitives in their flight by forging passes for slaves' (Foner, 1975c: 503).

Emancipation and Irish-America

Any such solidarity was dealt a severe blow by the emancipation of slaves. Freed blacks flocked north where they encountered large numbers of newly-arrived Irish immigrants escaping the Great Famine in Ireland. As they crowded into the cities of the east coast and mid-west – for example, 443 Irish immigrants entered Boston in 1836, and 65,556 a decade later (Foner, 1983: 214) – the Irish came face to face with black labourers and saw them immediately as competitors for their low status jobs.[18] Although the number of blacks initially represented little real economic threat, the Irish quickly targeted blacks as scapegoats. As early as 1850, the *New York Tribune* remarked on the paradox that the Irish who had recently escaped from bondage were at the forefront of opposition to rights for black people (Wittke, 1970: 125). Nor was the racism confined to the working class. John Mitchel's support for slavery has already been noted. Other Irish revolutionary exiles, such as Joseph Brenan and Thomas Meagher, expressed similar views (*ibid*: 126-7). And the American Catholic church, although officially neutral on the issue of slavery, was predominatly opposed to the emancipation of slaves. Tyrone-born Bishop John Hughes of New York opined that an abolitionist was also 'an anti-hanging man, women's rights man, an infidel frequently, bigoted Protestant always, a socialist, a red republican, a fanatical teetotaller ...' (*ibid*: 129). The *Catholic Telegraph* of Cincinnati was the only American Catholic paper of the period to take a consistent and principled stand against slavery.

As the opinions of Bishop Hughes indicate, the bulk of Irish immigrants were not at the forefront of abolitionism, dismissing it as being a product of rabid evangelical Protestantism. But they were ambivalent on a number of aspects of emancipation. For example, the creation of 30 black regiments within six months of the emancipation proclamation was opposed by some as tantamount to encouraging 'slave rebellions', while for others it was preferable that black soldiers rather than white march off to be killed. An Irish-American song of the era puts it thus (Litwack 1980: 71):

Some tell us 'tis a burnin shame to make the naygers fight;
An' that the thrade of bein' kilt belongs but to the white;
But as for me, upon my soul! So liberal are we here,
I'll let Sambo be murthered instead of myself on every day of the year.

The Irish community was not in favour of a war to coerce the South to abandon slavery, yet came to be among the foremost supporters of that war. They solved the dilemma involved by making it clear that they were fighting for the Union, not for emancipation. As one popular Irish poem of 1861 put it – referring to a prominent Irish-American anti-abolitionist, Stephen Douglas (Shannon, 1974: 56):

To the tenets of Douglas we tenderly cling,
Warm hearts to the cause of our country we bring;
To the flag we are pledged – all its foes we abhor –
And we ain't for the nigger but are for the war.

The Irish proved loyal to the Union, volunteering in droves and forming 38 Union regiments with the word 'Irish' in their title (*ibid*: 59). Yet the attempt to draft New York Irish immigrants into the army led to severe riots in July 1863. Admittedly, the Irish had some reason for frustration; anomalies in the draft procedure meant that the burden of the draft fell on them; this was corrected later. Moreover, as poor labourers, they could not find the $200 which could have bought them out of donning the uniform. At the same time, the targets for the violence quickly became almost solely black people and property. Of 82 rioters who died in the disturbances, 52 were Irish (Wood, 1970: 24).

This anti-black pogrom was only one of a number of the period in cities such as Milwaukee, Cincinnati (Wittke, 1970: 126) and Detroit (Katzman, 1973: 44). Irish labourers were in the vanguard at all the riots. The widespread nature of the disturbances reveals that what was at stake was not merely one localised instance of unfair procedures in drafting soldiers; rather, the riots represented the Irish working class' attempt to remove black competition for their jobs, in the process gaining respectability in white America.

Ignatiev (1995: 41) points out that 'the first Congress of the United States voted in 1790 that only "white" persons could be naturalized as citizens ... but ... it was by no means obvious who was "white". In the early years the Catholic Irish were shunned even more than the Scotch-Irish by WASP America and were frequently referred to as "niggers turned inside out"...' What changed is that the Irish became 'white', 'came to boast the white skin as their highest prerogative' (*ibid*: 69). With the crucial strategic backing of the Democratic Party eager for their vote, Irish labourers organised to exclude black people from their trades and professions. Irish-American labour associations 'denounced the abolitionists not for opposing slavery but for placing the cause of the slave ahead of the cause of the free worker' (*ibid*: 108). The Irish arrived at the politically empowering conclusion that they had to distance themselves as far as possible from slaves and black people in order to become upwardly mobile.

> To be acknowledged as white it was not enough for the Irish to have a competitive advantage over Afro-Americans in the labor market; in order for them to avoid the taint of blackness it was necessary that no Negro be allowed to work in occupations where Irish were to be found (*ibid*: 112).

They forced blacks out of numerous trades and occupations – house servant, cook, waiter, porter, longshoreman, labourer – and joined the white republic. As Frederick Douglass commented: 'Every hour sees the black man elbowed out of employment by some newly-arrived immigrant whose hunger and whose colour are thought to give him a better title to the place' (Foner, 1983: 214). One of the surest signs that they had arrived socially was when the first Irish policemen appeared on the streets – legally armed Irish Catholics in WASP America. The Irish had climbed the ladder by a rung or two, leaving the blacks at the bottom and justifying the arrangements by racist attitudes[19] which many black commentators found remarkable for their intensity and apparent incongruity. Frederick Douglass (1962: 546) concluded:

> Perhaps no class of our fellow-citizens has carried this prejudice against color to a point more extreme and dangerous than have our Catholic Irish fellow-citizens, and yet no people on the face of the earth have been more relentlessly persecuted and oppressed on account of race and religion than have this same Irish people.

Afro-American support for Ireland

Given the experience of Afro-Americans at the hands of Irish-Americans, Douglass' generosity of spirit is both noteworthy and emblematic. There is evidence of Afro-American intolerance of the Irish. For example, anti-Irish jokes became common among American blacks, with collections being gathered as early as

1870. These jokes often depicted the Irish man as lazy and incompetent and often involved the teller in mimicking an Irish accent. The jokes were an important means of 'laughing at the man' (Levine, 1977: 300) – that is, not just a reaction to treatment by the Irish in events like the New York Draft Riots of 1863, but also a means of getting back at whites in general. 'The Irish characters of black jokelore became surrogates for all the other whites against whom it could be dangerous to speak openly' (*ibid*: 302). The low status of the Irish made them the target least likely to have the power to object.

Beyond the jokes, there is evidence of more positive relations.[20] Afro-Americans, and in particular their leading thinkers and activists, frequently displayed adulation of and support for the Irish struggle for freedom despite what Irish-Americans had done to them. Thus, after emancipation and the Civil War, blacks met in each state of the Union to plan their future political progress. These formal State Conventions also discussed a wide range of matters pertaining to black people. The State Convention meeting in California on 27 October 1865 adopted the following resolution:

> Resolved – That we sympathize with the Fenian movement to liberate Ireland from the yoke of British bondage, and when we have obtained our full citizenship in this country, we should be willing to assist our Irish brethren in their struggle for National Independence; and 40,000 colored troops could be raised to butt the horns off the hypocritical English bull (Foner and Walker, 1980: 178).

Two decades later, in a speech to the Colored National League of Boston in March 1886, Edward Everett Brown, who established the first black law firm in Massachusetts, singled out the Irish anti-colonial struggle as the model to be followed by black Americans seeking liberation (Foner and Branham, 1998: 680-2). And in 1916, commenting on the Easter Rising in Dublin, the great black American William Du Bois said: 'The recent Irish revolt may have been foolish, but would to God some of us had sense enough to be fools' (Moses, 1978: 225). A. Philip Randolph, the black socialist, similarly saw the Irish struggle and that of Afro-Americans as parallel (*ibid*: 244-5).

Another black American socialist, Claude McKay, lived in London during a key period in Anglo-Irish relations – from the end of 1919 to the beginning of 1921. At the socialist International Club in London he met many political activists from throughout Europe, including Ireland (Fryer, 1984: 318-20). As Cooper (1987: 154) concludes, 'McKay loved the Irish. He considered them racially prejudiced, like other whites, but not hypocritical, like the Anglo-Saxons'. McKay wrote positively of the Irish revolution in articles such as 'How Black Sees Green and Red' in the *Liberator*, the socialist Afro-American periodical. At the same time, as a committed socialist, he was under no illusion about the socialist potential of Sinn Féin in 1921.[21]

The fault lines in Afro-American political thinking in the early decades of the 20th century were between nationalists and socialists, the latter tending to identify with Russia and the former with Ireland. The identification of the black nationalists with the Irish was not confined to words. Cyril V. Briggs, before espousing more socialist politics, had formed a secret society, the African Blood Brotherhood for African Liberation and Redemption, in 1919, modelled directly on the Irish Republican Brotherhood (Hill, 1983: lxxii). S.A.G. Cox, the founder of the National Club of Jamaica, had been a law student in London in 1905, the year Arthur Griffith formed Sinn Féin. Later in Jamaica Cox named his newspaper *Our Own*, a reference to the translation of 'sinn féin' – 'ourselves' (*ibid*: lxxiii).

The Assistant Secretary of the National Club of Jamaica at the time was Marcus Garvey, who later came to prominence through the United Negro Improvement Association (UNIA) in the United States and his 'Back to Africa' campaign. Garvey quite deliberately modelled his UNIA on similar developments by Irish activists. In 1919, he named the UNIA headquarters in New York Liberty Hall, in honour of the headquarters of James Connolly's

Irish Citizen Army in Dublin (*ibid*: lxxiv). In the same year he called for an 'International Convention of the Negro Peoples of the World', one week after 6000 Irish-Americans attended the third Irish Race Convention in Philadelphia (*ibid*: lxxv). That black Convention met in August 1920, and from it, Garvey sent a telegram to Eamon De Valera stating: 'We believe Ireland should be free even as Africa shall be free for the Negroes of the world' (*ibid*: lxxviii). Shortly afterwards Garvey attended a meeting of Irish longshoremen in Liberty Hall, New York to discuss a boycott of British ships in protest at the treatment of Terence MacSwiney, Lord Mayor of Cork, then on hunger strike in Britain. He told the longshoremen that he had sent a telegram to Father Dominick, the priest attending MacSwiney, offering the 'sympathy of 400,000,000 Negroes'.[22] After the meeting Garvey sent some of his colleagues to the New York docks to urge black longshoremen to support their Irish colleagues (*ibid*: lxxvi). Finally, when asked the significance of the UNIA's tricolour, Garvey replied: 'The Red showed their sympathy with the "Reds" of the world, and the Green their sympathy for the Irish in their fight for freedom, and the Black – The Negro' (*ibid*: lxxix).

Marcus Garvey

Garvey's admiration of and support for Irish liberation seems to have been rarely reciprocated. There is no record of De Valera having telegrammed Garvey urging black liberation as being on a par with Irish independence. And Arthur Griffith, recipient of another telegram from Garvey congratulating him on the Treaty negotiations – 'your masterly achievement of partial independence for Ireland' (*ibid*: lxxvii) – was not matched by anything approaching similar sentiments on Griffith's part. When writing the introduction to Mitchel's *Jail Journal* (1913), Griffith condemned the fact that in every generation there was 'an inky tribe of small Irishmen' who sought to attack Mitchel. He added:

> Even his views on Negro-slavery have been deprecatingly excused, as if excuse were needed for an Irish Nationalist declining to hold the Negro his peer in right. When the Irish Nation need explanation or apology for John Mitchel, the Irish nation will need its shroud (Mitchel, 1913: xiii-xiv).[23]

The Irish in Australia

In Australia, the path to respectability for Irish immigrants was more difficult and involved an intensely brutal relationship with the local black population. For some, the protection of property they owned or managed was reason enough to brutalise Aborigines. Take the example of Alexander Crawford, born in Belfast in 1857 and the older brother of Fred Crawford who later organised the Larne gun-running in 1912 to arm the Ulster Volunteer Force. By 1881 Alexander Crawford was managing a sheep station in the remote outback of Western Australia. There he quickly came to believe that sheep stealing by Aborigines was a serious threat not only to the owner's property, but also to his own ambitions to achieve fame and fortune. His response to sheep stealing involved a number of tactics. 'I have nine white men in the station and about 20 niggers, some I only keep and feed to keep them from stealing the sheep', he wrote in a letter to his fiancee Lillie in May 1882 (O'Farrell, 1984: 66-7). Another tactic was the pursuit and punishment of sheep-stealers, although it is clear from his letters than on such hunts it was not always certain if the Aborigines captured and beaten or jailed were in fact the culprits. He apologised to Lillie for the monotony of his letters: 'The only incidents that occur are nigger hunts' (*ibid*: 68). The letters also reveal that his antagonism towards the local population was more than tactical, that it was based in a deep-seated racism. He complained of their eating habits and sneered that their language – which he could not speak – was devoid of verbs and tenses. In their letters to him, both his fiancee and parents chided him. 'I hope you are getting on with the natives better, your Aunt Matty says kindness goes far with them', wrote his father (*ibid*: 73). And Lillie wrote:

> It is a dreadful thing to be continually hunting down one's fellow creatures, for they are our fellow creatures and have precious and immortal souls. Oh my darling keep your hands free from your fellow creature's blood (*ibid*: 76).

Compared to earlier Irish immigrants to Australia, Crawford undoubtedly had an easy passage. He was white and Protestant in a society where these attributes were central to social mobility. For the Irish who came in the first half of the 19th century, it was a different matter entirely. Between 1785 and 1850, beginning slowly in the first two decades, an estimated 150,000 men and women were transported from England and Ireland to penal colonies in Australia (Hughes, 1987: 161-2). The Irish among them were poor and Catholic, and although their labour was an essential element in the creation of the infrastructure of the new society, they were despised by the Protestant colonial aristocracy and military. Some of the Irish transportees were rebels who had planned or been engaged in political insurrection in Ireland – United Irishmen from 1798, Young Irelanders from 1848, and Fenians. They constituted only a minority of Irish transportees – less than 1500 in Hughes' (1987: 195) estimation. But the colonial administration was fearful of their presence to the point of paranoia. They were 'bearers of Jacobin contagion' (*ibid*: 181) who could revolt at any time. Nassau Senior – the economic advisor to the British government who at the time of the Great Famine felt that one million dead would hardly do much good – described the transportation of Irish political agitators as 'sowing our colonies with poisoned seed' (Tomlinson 1995: 196-7) That establishment paranoia was extended to all the Irish who were marked out for special treatment and brutality.

There was indeed an Irish revolt. In Paramatta on Sunday 4 March 1804, the Irish political prisoners revolted. Marching together singing the rebel song from 1798, 'The Croppy Boy', they armed themselves as best they could and burned some buildings. The rebellion did not last long. Within hours, military reinforcements had arrived. Fewer than 30 Botany Bay Rangers routed the 266 rebels within minutes at a hill which became known as Vinegar Hill – in memory of the hill in Wexford where other croppies had been slaughtered six years previously (*ibid*: 191-4). It was 'the last reverberation of 1798' (McDowell 1974: 53).

If the radical Jacobin fervour of such convicts was all there was to report about the Irish transportees, it would be possible to read their contribution to the development of Australian culture and politics solely as heroic and progressive. But there is another story to tell. 'Australian racism began with the convicts, although it did not stay confined to them for long; it was the first Australian trait to percolate upward from the lower class' (Hughes, 1987: 95). There were many reasons for hostility between the convicts and the Aborigines. At least in theory, in the early days the Aborigines had full legal status and the convicts did not – a major source of resentment on the part of the convicts. Also at an early stage convicts stole the few possessions of the Aborigines – tools and weapons – to sell to sailors as souvenirs, a reason for blacks to despise the convicts. Convicts who escaped to the bush frequently starved to death. Those who did not were in danger of attack by Aborigines or of being hunted down by the military led by expert black trackers. And finally, when convicts were freed, they had no money to buy property; relegated to the poorest land on the edge of European settlement or in the outback itself, and unable to afford weapons, they lived in constant fear and hatred of the Aborigine population. One of the clearest signs of this was their 'sport' of 'nigger hunting'. And the antagonism was mutual. Hughes (1987: 279) tells the tale of one missionary who in 1837 had blankets carefully sewn together as winter clothing for Aborigines. On a later visit he found they 'had unpicked all the stitches and turned them back into blankets, because they thought them "Irish cloaks" – "our natives commonly attach some idea of inferiority to what is Irish ...".' Perhaps the most telling sign of the gap that separated poor whites and poor blacks was that the badge of honour most coveted by the Irish political transportees and most feared by the white establishment – the title of 'croppy', derived from the Irish rebels' custom of cutting their hair short like French revolutionaries – was a badge of disdain as far as the blacks were concerned. When offered the left-over convict slops on one occasion, the Aborigines rejected them with the words, 'No good – all same like croppy' (*ibid*: 279).[24]

Bringing it all back home

Emigration, whether through transportation or economic necessity, was a central element in Irish society for centuries up to the final decades of the 20th century. In time, it encouraged the custom of the 'American wake' – a party for the departing emigrant who would never return, who would be gone as surely as if they had died. But of course, that was not the whole story. Some, especially those who had money to begin with or made their fortunes abroad, did return. And even if the poorer emigrants did not, they were not all illiterate; they wrote letters to family back in Ireland. Lastly, even in the absence of such direct contact, there was great interest in Ireland in news from the countries to which they went. This was particularly true of America in the late 18th century where news of the exciting political developments in terms of representation and democracy was consumed avidly by artisans and merchants in Ireland. As its name suggests, the *Belfast Newsletter*, founded in 1737 and committed to the radical Enlightenment cause, often received its news from the colonies not from its own employed correspondents but from emigrants on the spot. In this way the paper became the first in Europe to reproduce the American Declaration of Independence in 1776, which, incidentally, had been printed in Philadelphia by Samuel Dunlop from Strabane.

In all of these ways, people in Ireland who would never themselves set foot in America or Australia were informed of developments there and in the process learned to look on those societies through the eyes of their relatives and compatriots who reported back to them.

Take the case of emigrants' letters. We have already seen how Alexander Crawford's letters home spoke vividly of his relationship with the local population. As Green (1969) reveals, letters from Irish Protestant emigrants to America in the 18th century have also survived, even if not in vast numbers.[25] Many of these letters, but not all, were from the better educated, more middle class emigrants. For the most part, they are full of news about family and friends, as well as about religion. But they also give an insight into other issues and experiences, such as the hazardous experience of the Atlantic crossing, or the opportunities and setbacks encountered on the other side. They also undoubtedly gave people in Ireland who would never meet native Americans a vicarious sense of the pioneers' fear of them. Thus, although they have not survived, there must have been letters home such as those of James Magraw in 1733 to his brother. James was one of a small cluster of Scotch-Irish emigrants who had ventured into the wilderness of the Cumberland Valley to start a settlement; his brother lived in Paxtang, which by then was firmly settled by Europeans. James' letters tell of clearing land, of planting and hunting, and of fevers which claim the lives of young children. They also speak of his relationship with the native population. '... get some guns for us. There's a good wheen of injuns about here' (Fitzpatrick, 1989: 68). Through such contacts the Irish at home could learn to be racist.

5. Empire

The Wild Geese

For two centuries after the Flight of the Earls in 1607 countless Irishmen left their country and enlisted in the armies of Europe; there were perhaps as many as half a million of them in Europe in the 18th century (Karsten 1983: 32). Known as 'the Wild Geese', they were the cream of the Irish Catholic elite, forced abroad 'by their military defeats in Ireland, the ensuing social and economic deprivation of the plantations and related political and religious repression' (Murtagh, 1996: 294). The British government was more than pleased to be rid of these 'idle swordsmen' in Ireland, preferring to meet them in battle in continental Europe. On more than one occasion, the British went as far as shipping entire Irish regiments defeated in battle in Ireland to Europe.

The first major exodus was after the crushing of the Desmond rebellion in Munster in 1583 (for the details in the following paragraphs, see Murtagh, 1996: 295-305). The defeated Irish went to Spain, with at least 200 of them returning five years later with the doomed Armada. In 1605 the defeat at Kinsale led to another haemorrhage. The Irish soldiers who lost were relocated to Spanish Flanders where they formed an Irish regiment. There were at least another five Irish regiments in the service of Spain during the Thirty Years War. Over 30,000 defeated Irish soldiers left for Spain in the 1650s in the wake of Cromwell's campaign.

By this time Spain's power was waning and France's waxing, with the result that increasingly the Wild Geese went to France. There were seven Irish regiments in France, comprising at least 10,000 men, in 1635, and in 1691, following the Treaty of Limerick, British ships ferried a further 16,000 defeated Irish soldiers to France. After the French Revolution, Wild Geese flocked both to and from France. Exiled United Irishmen formed the Third Foreign Regiment under Napolean in 1803, while many existing Irish regiments in the French service went over to the British out of royalist sympathies.

The Irish migrated far and wide. There were over 100 Irish field marshals, generals and admirals under the Hapsburg monarchy from 1612 on. At least 6,000 Irish swordsmen served the Swedish monarch at the beginning of the 17th century, but defected to Germany and Poland, preferring Catholic to Protestant monarchs. And there were around 20 Irish officers in the Russian army in the 17th century.

The Wild Geese have gone down in Irish nationalist history as brave, disciplined and highly efficient soldiers who continued the war against England in other theatres. The success of Clare's Dragoons and other Irish regiments against the British at the Battle of Fontenoy in 1745 – where their war cry was, 'Remember Limerick and England's treachery!' – was custom-made for the heroic songs of balladeers like Thomas Davis a century later. But they did not only fight the British. As an officer for the Hapsburg monarchy, Francis Taafe, Fourth Earl of Carlingford, played a leading role in the campaign against the Turks in the 1680s. Irish regiments in the service of Spain fought in Flanders, Italy, Minorca, North Africa and Spanish America, including the Caribbean and Louisiana. As such, they played an essential role in the upholding of the Spanish empire, with its racism and oppression of people of colour. The Irish became implicated in this oppression.

Take the case of Randell Mac Donnell in the late 17th century (McDonnell, 1996: 53-58). A Catholic and descendant of Sorley Boy Mac Donnell, Earl of Antrim, who had rebelled against the English, he nevertheless joined the British navy at a time when technically it was barred to Catholics. He was sent to a squadron protecting Tangiers, a colony which King Charles II of England had acquired as part of his wife's dowry. He proved adept at capturing Moorish pirate ships and their cargoes and was quickly promoted. He was given the responsibility of bringing a Moorish ambassador and his company to England for peace talks between Charles II and the Sultan of Morocco. The peace process later collapsed, and Mac Donnell was put in charge of a frigate in a war with the Sultan. He eventually became commander of the 'Moroccan' squadron. His loyalty to the English monarchy meant that when James II decided to escape from England ahead of Prince William of Orange's advance on London, Mac Donnell was given the responsibility of getting the Queen and her baby to safety in France. He smuggled

Rose O'Neill and Henry O'Neill
(see note 27, page 94)

them out of Gravesend in a rowing boat to a waiting ship, with the Queen disguised as a laundress. He returned to rescue James, bringing the disguised King to France in a rickety old fishing boat.

In the midst of all these adventures, Randell Mac Donnell had time for slave trading[26] and with the money he gained from this lucrative source later bought land near Ballymoney, County Antrim. He sold a black slave to Charles II for £50. Charles presented the slave to his French mistress, Louise de Quérouailles, whose maid-in witting, a Tipperary woman named Hannah Roche, was Randell's wife (for a portrait of Louise accompanied by the slave, see McDonnell, 1996: 45).[27]

Serving the British Empire

Technically only Protestants could hold commissions in the British forces prior to a relief act of 1793, when the British decided that the fear of a French invasion was more pressing than the continuation of penal laws against Catholics. However, as the case of Randell Mac Donnell reveals, some did manage to circumvent that ban, especially in the navy where it seemed to be less rigorously applied. Moreover, there was nothing to prevent Irish Protestants becoming officers prior to 1793, nor indeed Irish Catholics joining the forces of the Crown as rank and file soldiers and seamen. Thus in 1771 the 15th Foot Regiment was almost entirely Catholic, while at the same time perhaps half of the private army of the East India Company was Catholic (Karsten, 1983: 56-7). In the 18th century, this trend continued, with the additional factor that Catholics could now be officers. By 1830 Irish men constituted 42 percent of the British Army at a point when the Irish made up 32 per cent of the United Kingdom population overall. That disproportionate representation persisted even after the devastation of the Famine on the Irish population; in 1881 21 percent of the British Army was Irish while 15 per cent of the United Kingdom population was Irish (Jeffery, 1996b: 94-5). Twelve per cent of naval officers between 1793 and 1815 were

Irish, as were one quarter of the seamen with Nelson at Trafalgar (McDowell 1974: 58). In the early 1880s 30 per cent of surgeons in the British Army were Irish (*ibid*: 62).

Thus, Irish names abound in the military history of India. At the Battle of Pondicherry in 1761, the French forces under Galway man Thomas Lally were defeated by British forces under the command of Limerick man Eyre Coote (Kapur, 1997: 4). William Henry Tone, brother of Wolfe Tone, was a colonel in the service of an Indian ruler and died in battle (*ibid*: 5). John Lawrence from Derry was at the forefront of the suppression of the Indian Mutiny in 1857 (*ibid*: 17).

For the Catholic working class, service to the Empire, especially in the army, was a way out of poverty.

> The Irish soldier among Britain's 'regulars', then, was typically a Catholic, but a Catholic of low income, poorer than those who took up arms against Britain [in Ireland] from time to time and poorer than those who did not serve (Karsten, 1983: 37).

Irish involvement was not confined to the British Army, however. Hence in 1857, when Ireland's population was 30 percent of that of the United Kingdom, Irish universities supplied 33 percent of Indian Civil Service recruits (Kapur, 1997: 6). In the 1890s, seven of the eight provinces of India were government by Irish men (*ibid*). As Fraser (1996: 77) concludes, 'Ireland helped sustain the British Raj in India out of all proportion to her size'. Nor was this conclusion confined to India; Irish men played key administrative and military roles throughout the British Empire at its height.

The British Empire offered opportunity for the Irish middle class, Catholic and Protestant, each for its own reason.

> Of all the categories of Irish people for whom the Empire provided opportunities, perhaps it was the declining Ascendancy class who benefited most, finding a raison d'être in imperial service progressively denied to them at home... While imperial service might shore up the

precarious finances of a declining social group, it could also boost the fortunes of the rising Catholic middle class (Jeffery, 1996a: 17).

Throughout the British Empire, where there were military campaigns, defeated local forces, repression, massacre and racism, the chances were that Irish people were centrally involved in designing, administering or enforcing British rule – generals and rank and file soldiers, governors and clerks. Tens of thousands of Irish people encountered people of colour across the globe as an integral part of the conquering and ruling force, thereby determining the one-sided nature of their relationship with the vanquished and the ruled. Objectively, as Irish people, they could be said to have shared an experience of defeat and oppression with local people they met in India, Africa and elsewhere, but the reality was that their intimate involvement in the running of the Empire meant there was often little chance of them seeing what they shared with those they helped oppress. To take just one example of many: Sir Michael O'Dwyer from Tipperary was Lieutenant-Governor of the Punjab in April 1919 when a British unit under the command of Brigadier-General Reginald Dyer (born in India of an Irish father, and educated in Cork) opened fire without warning on an unarmed crowd in Amritsar, the holy city of the Sikhs; officially 379 people died (the real death toll is likely to have been closer to 600) and another 1,200 were injured. O'Dwyer had not authorised Dyer's action, but rushed to voice his approval of it. The Sikhs eventually had their revenge when Ud Lam Singh assassinated O'Dwyer in London in 1940 (Fraser, 1996: 88-9; Kapur, 1997: 34-36).

The loyalty of such Irishmen was beyond question. In fact, at times it was judged that as Irishmen they were more able to guarantee colonial rule. Thus, Lord Dufferin from County Down was Viceroy of India in 1885 when the Indian National Congress was formed. He immediately drew parallels with Home Rule agitation in Ireland and warned that some decisive action was necessary if India was to avoid Irish-style political unrest (Kapur,

1997: 14). Another example is that of Sir Charles Tegart, police commissioner of Calcutta, an Irishman, born in County Meath, the son of a Church of Ireland minister. He was known for his ruthless suppression of Bengali revolutionary nationalists at the beginning of the 20th century (who incidentally drew their inspiration from Irish nationalists). When Tegart was honoured by the Caledonian Society of Calcutta in 1924, one speaker summed up succinctly the imperial value of such Anglo-Irish functionaries: 'I always think an Irishman is specially suited to be a policeman. Being by instinct "agin the government" he knows exactly what people who want to make trouble feel like and is able to forestall their action' (quoted in Silvestri, 2000: 40).

The same presumptions did not apply to Irish Catholics. Before Irish Catholics were officially allowed into the British armed forces, the fear was always that they would prove disloyal, a fifth column undermining the institution from within. In the 18th and especially 19th century Irish revolutionaries attempted to capitalise on that possibility by infiltrating the British Army. The United Irishmen did it, as did the Fenians over half a century later. John Devoy, the Fenian leader, claimed that up to one-third of the British troops garrisoned in Ireland had taken the Fenian oath (Karsten 1983: 46). It is difficult to ascertain the exact accuracy of this claim, but the more important point is about the effects of this infiltration – or rather, the lack of such effects. There was no mutiny or uprising within the British Army at this time, whatever the extent of Fenian penetration.

During World War I Sir Roger Casement attempted a variation on the Fenian theme. He had himself been a functionary of the British Empire, as British Consul to Portuguese West Africa. While there he had investigated and campaigned against the brutal treatment of the local population by the Belgians in the Congo.[28] At the end of 1914, John Devoy and Clan na Gael in America sent him to Germany with three purposes: to secure German military help in the event of a rising in Ireland, to educate German public opinion about Ireland, and to organise

Irish prisoners of war into a military force to fight for Irish freedom (Inglis 1993: 291). He was doomed to failure in the last of these. The Irish prisoners had already expressed their loyalty clearly. When conditions were improved for them at Senelager, the camp where most of them were held, they protested that they

Roger Casement

wanted no better treatment than that meted out to other prisoners; 'In addition to being Irish Catholics, we have the honour to be British soldiers' (*ibid*: 300). When Casement went to another camp, Limburg, to recruit, he appears to have been jostled and pushed; he managed to convince no more than a handful to switch allegiance. In the end, Casement's plans, though heartfelt and idealistic, were rejected not just by the Irish prisoners he hoped to muster, but also by John Devoy and the Clan who had sent him. Devoy was totally opposed to Casement's proposal that if the Irish Brigade which he hoped to raise could not be sent to Ireland, then they should fight alongside the Turks against the British in Egypt. 'A blow struck at the British invaders of Egypt, to aid Egyptian national freedom, is a blow struck for a kindred cause to that of Ireland' (*ibid*: 309).

In World War I Irish men in the British Army thus proved no less loyal than their predecessors had in the 19th century. A prime case in point is that of the Royal Munster Rifles (Dooley, 1998). The Regiment's origins are in the private army formed by the East India Company in 1652. In 1861, this army was transferred to the British Crown and in 1881 was retitled the Royal Munster Fusiliers. During World War I they fought in Gallipoli and were later transferred to France. Two days after the Easter Rising in Dublin, they were taunted by the Germans in the opposite trenches, who displayed placards reading: 'Irishmen! Heavy uproar in Ireland; english guns are firing at your wives and children!'[29] The Fusiliers responded by singing Irish songs and 'Rule Britannia', and by crawling across to the German trenches to seize the offending placards. This was perhaps unsurprising behaviour from a regiment, one of whose number had assaulted Roger Casement in 1914 when he tried to recruit prisoners of war for an Irish Regiment. True, when the war ended, a few of the Munster Fusiliers broke ranks. Some gave their rifles to republicans when they returned to Ireland and one, Joseph O'Sullivan from Bantry, was one of the IRA assassins of General Sir Henry Wilson, former Chief of Imperial Staff and himself a southern Irish Protestant, in London in June 1922; O'Sullivan was one of two men hanged for this. But these were exceptions to the rule: the Regiment had displayed almost unblemished loyalty over two and a half centuries of imperial service.

One other exception to the rule of loyalty stands out: the mutiny of 61 members of the Connaught Rangers in India in 1922, in protest at the repression in Ireland being carried out by the British auxiliaries, the Black and Tans. One of the mutineers, Private Jim Daly, was executed by a firing squad comprised of colleagues from his own regiment (Karsten, 1983: 49). Heroic as this gesture may have been, it has to be seen in the context of the times. During the War of Independence in Ireland, 1919-21, Irish men continued to enlist in the British Army; in fact, they did so at twice the pre-war rate (*ibid*: 49). It is probable that 'most were no more political than most of the very poor of any other land' (*ibid*: 41). Their loyalty was never in doubt. Consequently they were unlikely to see the similarity between what the British Empire had done to their country and what they were doing in the Empire's name to oppress others. There was little chance of them finding common cause with people of colour in the Empire. On the contrary, they were likely to return to Ireland with tales of heroic conquests and massacres and thus pass on racist views to others who had never met people of colour.

Resisting the Empire

That said, the actions of Joseph O'Sullivan and Jim Daly, though a minority response to the experience of empire, did represent a tradition of resistance to empire, some of it from within. Thus, Kiernan (1969: 28) recounts that 'Irish employees in Scotland Yard are said to have aided Indian nationalists to smuggle their literature'. Much more public was the attempt by Michael Davitt, a member of the 11-man Supreme Council of the Irish Republican Brotherhood, to use the international connections within the British Empire for anti-imperialist purposes. He campaigned unsuccessfully to have Dadabhai Naoroji, an Indian resident in London, returned to the British parliament from an Irish constituency in order 'to give a direct voice in the house of commons to Indian nationalism…' (Moody, 1981: 549). In this sense, he was following in the footsteps of Daniel O'Connell who in 1839 was one of the founders of the British India Society which sought to focus attention on the abuses carried out by the East India Company (Fraser, 1996: 85).

Irish anti-imperialist solidarity was not confined to India. In 1879 the Irish Republican Brotherhood sought to send 20,000 dollars and a few military strategists to the Zulus to help them rise up against British rule. In answer to objections, the main proposer of the scheme, J.J. O'Kelly argued: '...the English will find it much more difficult to fight one hundred thousand Kaffirs in their immense and practically unknown country than they would the same number of Irishmen in a little Island where every nook and corner is known and which is cut up in all directions by practicable roads... one million cartridges placed in the hands of the Zulus would help the Irish cause more than an equivalent amount of arms landed in Ireland' (O'Brien and Ryan, 1979: 410).

While such support was clearly not totally altruistic it nonetheless contributed to the reputation of Irish radicals as anti-colonialist and internationalist, a reputation not lost on those struggling against British rule in Africa and Asia. Indian nationalists who founded the Congress Party in 1885 – such as Surendranath Banerjee – drew inspiration from the Irish Land League and in particular its tactic of boycotting (Kruger, 1975: 305). There were close contacts between Irish and Indian nationalists. The traffic in ideas and support was two-way. Irish woman Annie Besant was one of the founders of India's Home Rule movement in 1916 and was later President of the Indian National Congress (Kapur, 1997: 21-23). And Maud Gonne was involved in an attempt to rescue militant Indian nationalist Veer Savarleer from Brixton Jail in 1910 (*ibid*: 33).

Indian nationalists identified with Ireland's independence struggle. The Irish-American paper, *The Gaelic American*, frequently supported the Indian nationalist cause. Copies circulated widely in India itself, to the point that in October 1907, the British authorities banned its importation and sale (Kruger, 1975: 308). Jawaharlal Nehru, later the first prime minister of India, recalled that as a student in England he had visited Ireland where he had been impressed by the ideas of Sinn Féin (Jeffery 1996a: 9). After the 1916 Rising, in sentiments similar to those of Afro-American William Du Bois, Nehru wrote: 'But was that not true courage, which mocked at almost certain failure, and proclaimed to the world that no physical might could crush the invincible spirit of a nation' (quoted in Kapur, 1997: 38). V.V. Giri, President of India from 1969 to 1974, studied law at University College Dublin between 1915 and 1925 and was deported to India because of his close links with Irish republicans (*ibid*).

Interestingly, the identification with politics in Ireland was not confined to Indian nationalists. Jinnah, leader of the Muslims, who advocated partition and the creation of Pakistan, frequently noted the similarities between his cause and that of the Ulster unionists. He argued that Indian Muslims deserved at least as much in terms of political concessions from the British as did the unionists in Ireland and was supported in the British parliament by leading Ulster unionist, Sir Edward Carson (*ibid*: 34).

Frederick Engels wrote: 'Give me 200,000 Irishmen and I could overthrow the British Empire' (Marx and Engels, 1978: 43).[30] Unfortunately, the historical fact is that that number of Irishmen – and more – as soldiers and administrators kept the British Empire alive. Moreover, unlike many other Irish emigrants, they returned to Ireland where their tales of campaigns and sieges, massacres and uprisings undoubtedly served to import a particular view of people of colour into Irish popular culture.

The symbols of that Empire and its conquests remain throughout Ireland, whether in street names such as Sevastopol Street in Belfast, or public monuments such as that to the Irish-born Marquess of Dufferin, 1826-1902, former Viceroy of India, whose statue holds pride of place in the grounds of Belfast's City Hall, and portrays a subservient Indian prince. A similar prince appears in a number of banners carried by Lodges of the Orange Order on the Twelfth of July (see front cover). A kneeling Indian prince is shown receiving the bible from the hands of Queen Victoria; belief in the bible is thus said to be 'the secret of England's greatness', but there is no doubt that the subjugation of native peoples is also portrayed as being central to the imperial project.[31]

The missions: a religious empire

There was, of course, one sense in which the Irish did have their own empire – a religious one. During the 19th and 20th centuries, Irish Catholic[32] priests, nuns and brothers left to spread the Gospel throughout the world, particularly in Africa. In Nigeria by the middle of the 20th century, for example, they ran almost 2,500 primary schools with over half a million pupils, and almost 50 hospitals with three quarters of a million patients (Staunton, 2000: 44). At its height, missionary activity involved one in every 120 Irish adults (*ibid*).

Unlike the Spanish missionaries in South America, they did not directly represent the religious wing of military conquest. In fact, many found themselves, especially in Australasia and Africa, in the paradoxical position of being Irish nationalists whose presence required the sanction of British militarists and administrators. Their relationship with the British Empire was thus symbiotic. As a result, their spiritual mission often meshed neatly with the needs of the British authorities. For example, when Wexford-born Bishop Ricards in South Africa in 1853 came up with a plan to establish communities of monks among the African population in the hope of evangelising them, the British governor, Sir Bartle Frere, agreed on the grounds that 'the bishop's project was the first, best and most likely to be successful of all the plans submitted for the civilization of the Kaffir tribes' (Doyle, 1971: 17). A century later, seminarians being trained by the Holy Ghost Fathers for the missions of Nigeria were still being taught the correct protocols on being introduced to the Governor and his Lady (Coogan, 2000: 510). On the other hand, the effect of the missionaries' work was not unmitigatingly controlling. They played a key role in many countries in Africa in particular in providing health care and education. In the latter role, they were instrumental in the emergence of a new generation of educated Africans committed to anti-colonial struggle – Tom Mboya, Robert Mugabe, Julius Nyerere and Hastings Banda, to name a few.

Their effects were thus mixed. In South Africa, for example, Bishop Ricards proposed the introduction of apartheid at an early stage of British colonisation (Doyle, 1971: 13), and the Catholic Church 'cannot be said to have distinguished itself in universally outspoken condemnation of apartheid' (Coogan, 2000: 551) when it eventually emerged. At the same time, the Catholic church was one of the few (along with the Seventh Day Adventists and the United Jewish Reformed Congregation) to refuse to hand over their schools to Verwoerd's government in 1953 and instead 'soldiered on without state aid' (Mandela, 1994: 156).

Such a massive involvement of Irish people in missionary activity could not but have profound effects on Irish popular culture back home. And in this respect, the effect seems to have been much less ambivalent. Africa in particular came to be seen as a passive continent, its people 'as much in need of the civilizing influence of the Irish religious as parched earth was of water' (Coogan, 2000: 508). Nowhere was this more obvious than in relation to 'the black babies'. Generations of school children, north and south, were encouraged to donate money for the support of the missions. As Frank McCourt (1996: 119) recalls, this obligation was enforced, as so much of religion at the time, through appealing to fear and guilt rather than generosity. As his teacher reminded him, to forget the donation was to leave

> those little black pagans doomed forever for lack of baptism and knowledge of the True Faith[?] … Limbo is packed with little black babies flying around and crying for their mothers because they'll never be admitted to the ineffable presence of Our Lord …[33]

6. Visitors

Blacks in 18th century Ireland

The Irish who never left also had the opportunity to meet people of colour in their own country. Hart attempts to calculate how many black people there were in Ireland in the 18th century and in doing so uncovers a little-known phenomenon. There were, he estimates, between 2,000 and 3,000 black people, and continues: 'This is a tiny figure in relation to the population of the island as a whole, but it is as large as the recorded numbers of black people in France which had a population four times that of Ireland, and within Europe it is likely to have been exceeded only in England and perhaps in Spain or Portugal' (Hart, n.d: 3). Not surprisingly, the black population was concentrated in Dublin which had, 'with the exception of London, the largest black population of any 18th century European city' (*ibid*: 4).

There were, as we have seen, black soldiers in Ireland, some of whom may have stayed. The ports could also attract black seamen who could settle there, even if temporarily, and add to the mixed-race population of those cities and towns.[34]

There were also servants and slaves. Officially, just as Ireland did not participate in the slave trade, then slaves were not bought and sold within the country. But that did not prevent them arriving with sea captains, merchants, adventurers and returning soldiers, as was also the case in England. Already by the end of the 16th century it had become customary for titled and propertied families in England to have black slaves. One of the first to do so was Lady Raleigh, wife of Sir Walter (Fryer, 1984: 9). Although there is no evidence to this effect, it is tempting to believe that the Raleighs brought such black slaves with them when Walter was granted 42,000 acres of land in County Cork as a plantation in the 1580s. A century later, the possession of a black slave was as much a fashion statement of the rich of Ireland as those of England, so much so that the *Dublin Journal* of August 1783 criticised the 'preposterous Predilection for Exotics', and condemned those who preferred 'sooty-bottomed' foreigners to 'fair complexioned' Irish servants (quoted in Hart, n.d: 5).

The newspapers of the time give us some glimpse of the pervasiveness of this fashion. Sometimes the reference is positive, such as the death notice for Robert St George, 'a black', carried in the *Limerick Chronicle* of 27 July 1803. As Curtin (1999) makes clear, this unusual acknowledgement of a slave derives from the fact that nine years previously he had driven off robbers from his master's house, killing one in the process. Although there is no evidence of public slave markets in Ireland, the newspapers reveal that slaves were undoubtedly bought and sold (see Hart: 5 for a number of examples).

The newspapers also contained advertisements for runaway slaves. 'Run away from the service of Mrs Fullerton of Carrickfergus, on Sunday last, a negro slave boy...' (*Belfast Newsletter*, 14 June 1762; cited by Hart, n.d.). 'Run-away from Captain Tate of Sprucefield [Lisburn], on Thursday last, a black Boy, aged about 14 or 15 years. He is a Native of Bengal ...' (*Belfast Newsletter*, 25 September 1767; cited in Kapur, 1997: 50). What seems to come through from a number of these notices is that it was not the escape per se which was most aggravating to slave owners, but the fact that their 'property' had been 'stolen' by another. Thus *Faulkner's Dublin Journal* of 5 May 1767: 'On 30 April a black Indian girl the property of Andrew Armstrong, King's Co. was stolen or seduced away by one Patrick Comerford, an apprentice to Michael Ferns, house-painter. Any person who shall discover her shall get 2 guineas ... unless Comerford gives up the said girl he will be prosecuted with the utmost vigour' (cited in *Fernbane Parish and its Churches*, 1979: 66). Hart (n.d: 6-7) concludes: 'The boundaries between slave and non-slave in Ireland were not sharply defined... there was nothing uniquely oppressive or irremediable about the status of a slave in Ireland at this time ... it shaded into other categories of dependent status ...' The evidence is fairly compelling. Black people seem to have experienced little racial harassment, and it is clear that marriage with white people and the right to vote were not unknown. In fact, the attempt by a black servant of the Earl of Granard in 1783 to be allowed to vote was almost thwarted not because of the colour of his skin but because he had married a Catholic! (see Hart, n.d: 19). Yet, it is probably advisable not to make too much of the relatively comfortable existence of Irish slaves. No matter the privileges they in fact accessed, it cannot have been lost on the native Irish that such benefits resulted from largesse rather than right. In a situation where black people were bought and sold, and in the last analysis – surely the clearest sign of slavery – not paid for their labour, the conditions existed to nurture the roots of racism deep in Irish popular culture.

Freak shows and minstrels

Racist attitudes were confirmed in other ways in 18th and 19th century Ireland, not least by the frequent presence of black entertainers. At the lower end of the entertainment hierarchy was the freak show which paraded people with disabilities for the public's voyeuristic pleasure. One of the most poignant of these 'exhibits' was a young South African woman named Saartjie Baartman, better known in the freak shows as 'the Hottentot

Venus'. She appeared in London for the first time in 1810, exhibited by her two 'minders', Alexander Dunlop and Henrick Caesar. She had an extraordinarily large posterior which was successfully marketed by these two men as the object of great curiosity. When her story eventually became known as a result of a court case, it transpired that she was an orphan who had become a nursery maid in Henrick Caesar's household. He had brought her to England, where she had danced and otherwise performed in thin clothing so that the deformed shape of her body could be plainly seen. Abolitionists approached the English courts seeking a writ of Habeas Corpus on the grounds that she was being kept against her will. The court appointed someone to investigate her circumstances. His findings were that she had agreed with Caesar to allow herself to be exhibited for six years in return for half the profits. On this basis, the writ of Habeas Corpus was refused.

Whatever Caesar's promises, Saartjie seems to have seen little of any profit accrued. She ended up in Paris, in the keep of an animal showman, and died in May 1816, probably as the result of excessive drinking. She was probably not yet 30 years of age. The final ignominy was that she was allowed little peace even in death; a plaster cast of her body, along with her skeleton, are in the possession of the Musee de l'Homme in Paris (Edwards and Walvin, 1983: 171).[35]

During her sojourn in London, Saartjie Baartman was also exhibited in Ireland. In April 1812 she was in the city of Limerick. Lenihan (1967: 416) briefly but pointedly refers to her visit: '… she remained in Limerick five days, and much to the credit of the people, was visited by very few'. On this occasion at least it seems she was not the only one who failed to profit financially from her misfortune.

Much more commonplace in the mid-19th century were the black minstrel shows which were very popular and were covered widely in the press. Most, but not all, of these minstrel groups were blackface rather than genuine black performers, though there were performances by actual African tribesmen and native Americans in Dublin in the 1840s. Dublin attracted all the major minstrel acts of the day, including one of the most famous, the Christy Minstrels. But the craze was not confined to Dublin. Riach (1973: 235 and 241) notes the appearance of a group of women singers, the Female American Serenaders, who performed in Belfast in 1849 and the objections of some Presbyterian ministers in Derry to the Fisk Jubilee Singers including the song 'John Brown's Body' in their repertoire. Finally, there were also some black actors – such as Ira Aldridge (see Riach, 1973: 238-240) – and singers – such as Rachel Baptist (see Hart, n.d: 13-15).

But it was the blackface minstrel groups which proved the most popular, so much so that even an accomplished actor like Aldridge was frequently interrupted by audiences demanding that he sing minstrel songs, the presumption being that he must be made-up rather than genuinely black-skinned. The minstrel acts were taken to be authentic in their portrayal of black American slaves as the object of either fun or pity. The fun was based on their burlesque routines – what the *Freeman's Journal* referred to as their 'nigger comicality' (Riach, 1973: 234) – while the pathos related to the misery of slavery. That said, there was little evidence of condemnation of slavery in either the songs of the minstrels or the glowing tributes in the pages of Irish newspapers. Perhaps this more than even the easy use of racist language points to the extent to which racism had become assimilated into Irish popular culture.

Perhaps remarkably this blinkered approach to slavery is also obvious in the writing of one of the most enlightened authors of the period, Maria Edgeworth. Although able to condemn Irish landlordism, her conclusions about slavery were much more insipid. A collection of children's tales she published in 1802 contains the story of 'The Grateful Negro'. It is set in Jamaica and sets up two groups of opposing figures, the kind master and the cruel one, the grateful slave and the ungrateful one. The ungrateful slave Hector organises a slave revolt against the kind master, Mr Edwards, and Caesar, the grateful slave, dies defending his master's plantation. The moral at the end of Edgeworth's story is that as well as being aware of 'the treachery of the whole race of slaves, our readers ... will think that at least one exception may be made, in favour of THE GRATEFUL NEGRO' (quoted in Lively, 1998: 80).[36]

Surprisingly, the abolitionists of the time did not see that combating racism required criticism of racist portrayals of black people in the minstrel acts. Riach's (1973: 241) explanation for this is that 'these abolitionists were usually middle-class dissenters, and the same high-minded principles that led them into the movement to free the slave also led them to ignore the music hall as something unworthy'. Yet, the power of the images cannot be underestimated. Not only did it feed indigenous racism in Ireland, but it was 'carried to America in the minds of countless Irish emigrants'. As such, these emigrants were already programmed to endorse American racism.

One of the most prolific writers of songs for the minstrel genre was the American Stephen Foster, whose great grandfather had emigrated from Derry. One of Foster's songs is called 'No! My Nigger, no!' and contains the following lines:

> Dis you eber hear de coon preach on abolition?
> No, my nigger, no!
> (quoted in Riach, 1973: 233).

The fact is, however, that there were in Ireland at the same time of the minstrels genuine black abolitionists.

Visiting abolitionists

Anti-slavery activity was widespread in Ireland, not only in Dublin, but also in other towns and cities. In 1791-2 an ambitious boycott of slave-grown sugar (the antisaccharite movement) was organised in England, a highly innovative move considering that it involved consumers and in particular women. At its height, it

Charles Lenox Remond

was claimed that 300,000 families were involved, not merely in England, but also in urban centres in Ireland (Drescher, 1986: 78-9). The Hibernian Anti-Slavery Society was founded in Dublin in 1837 (Rice, 1981: 92-3). Undoubtedly the most prominent abolitionist in that city was Richard Davis Webb, a printer and publisher, and a Quaker. He edited the *Anti-Slavery Advocate* and was a regular contributor to the *American Anti-Slavery Standard*. Gathered around him was a group of people who delighted in the label of 'anti-everythingarians' – anti-vivisectionists, vegetarians and abolitionists.

Impressive public meetings were held in Dublin, Belfast and elsewhere to highlight the abolitionist message. Among the most impressive of those meetings were those addressed by black abolitionists from the United States, including former slaves. Often the Irish venues of these speakers were added on to their lecture tours in Britain. Thus, during his 17-month stay in Britain, Charles Lenox Remond lectured in 1841 in Dublin, Wexford, Waterford, Limerick, County Clare and Belfast.

Remond (1810-1873) was the son of a prosperous black businessman from Salem, Massachusetts, 'the first black Abolitionist speaker to address large audiences and the best known before the emergence of Frederick Douglass (Foner, 1975b: 508).[37] He enjoyed his time in Ireland immensely. He wrote from Dublin on 2 October 1841:

> ... Ireland ... is capable of exerting an influence more direct & important [,] more open & important than thousands of intelligent people have been wont to imagine. I have visited some six or seven important cities & towns in Ireland. In all of [them] I have held Anti American Slavery meetings and never in my life have I seen deeper interest Exhibited in proportion as the Irish people become Enlightened (Ripley, 1985: 97).

It was Remond who carried the 'Great Irish Address' (a petition organised by Daniel O'Connell, with 60,000 signatures of Irish people urging Irish Americans to oppose slavery) back to the United States in 1841.

Charles Lenox Remond's sister, Sarah Parker Remond, also visited Ireland. She had come to England originally in 1859 to give a series of lectures against slavery, but stayed on to get an education. She finally became a nurse and moved to Italy. In 1860 she spoke at a number of venues in Ireland. By all accounts an impressive speaker, she stressed the sexual exploitation of black women slaves and highlighted the problems facing black Americans freed from slavery (Midgely, 1992: 143-5; Fryer, 1984: 435).

As Ripley (1985: 332) concludes, 'several black lecturers discovered that an Irish tour could rejuvenate a flagging British anti-slavery mission'. Among such lecturers was Edmund Kelly, born in Columbia, Tennessee in 1817, the son of an Irish man and a slave woman. He later escaped from slavery and became a Baptist preacher in New Bedford, Massachusetts. In 1852 he went to England to try to raise the money necessary to buy the freedom of himself and his family. He raised £237 in London, Leeds and

Bristol, enough to free his family, but still needed £166 for his own manumission. On 7 April 1853 he addressed a large audience at a Baptist chapel in Lower Abbey Street, Dublin where he raised the remainder of the money he needed (*ibid*: 332-4).

Another black visitor around the same time was William G. Allen. He spent six months lecturing in Ireland and towards the end of his stay, on 23 November 1855, spoke in Downpatrick, County Down.[38] Allen later became the principal of a school in Islington, the first black school principal in England (Fryer, 1984: 434).

Frederick Douglass and Daniel O'Connell

By far the most prestigious of the black abolitionists to visit Ireland was Frederick Douglass. An escaped slave who, like Edmund Kelly, lived in New Bedford, Massachusetts, he spent two years lecturing in Britain and Ireland. An impressive orator, he had also written a best-selling autobiography, *Narrative of the Life of Frederick Douglass, an American Slave*. In 1845 Douglass came to Dublin where Richard Davis Webb had agreed to publish the British edition of his autobiography. He travelled widely in Ireland and spoke in Dublin, Cork, Limerick and Belfast. Douglass was only 27 years old at the time. Although this was his first trip to Ireland, strangely the Irish had figured in key points in his earlier life. When he was about 12, he read a book called *The Columbian Orator* (Boston 1797). Edited by Caleb Bingham, it contained extracts from speeches by people such as George Washington and William Pitt. Douglass was particularly impressed by one of the entries in the book, a speech by Richard Brinsley Sheridan – the Irish playwright, politician and orator, a staunch supporter of causes such as the freedom of the press – in support of Catholic emancipation in Ireland. 'What I got from Sheridan', he says, 'was a bold denunciation of slavery and a powerful vindication of human rights' (Douglass, 1971: 67). Around the same time Douglass encountered two

Irishmen unloading a barge at the docks in Baltimore, Maryland. One of the Irishmen asked him if he was a slave for life, and when he was told this was so, 'seemed to be deeply affected by the statement'. Both men advised him to run away to the north and freedom. 'From that time I resolved to run away', he concludes (*ibid*: 69).

Daniel O'Connell and Frederick Douglass

There was another Irishman who came to have a profound influence on Frederick Douglass – Daniel O'Connell. O'Connell took a principled stand on slavery even at the cost of weakening the support for his specifically Irish causes, Catholic Emancipation, and the Repeal of the Act of Union.[39] In the British House of Commons he refused the support of twenty MPs with interests in the West Indies in return for ceasing his attacks on slavery (Riach, 1980: 177). As one of the leading figures in the British abolitionist lobby, he did not drop the issue after abolition had been achieved, but, to the delight of American campaigners, switched his focus to the removal of American slavery. He became 'the single most important supporter that American anti-slavery had in Europe' (Riach, 1976: 24).

One of his rallying calls was the demand to 'send back the money' collected for the Repeal movement if it had been donated by slave owners. In reality, this tactic proved somewhat more rhetorical than real. There is only one known instance of him returning money – namely the sum of £178-14s-9d to New Orleans, not on abolitionist grounds but because those who sent it sought to pressure him to abandon his commitment to non-violence (*ibid*: 14). In effect, O'Connell accepted money from the Southern states provided it was not sent with the proviso that he tone down his outspoken stance on slavery. That said, there is no doubt that even a rhetorical commitment to sending back the money was highly influential, not least, as we shall see, on the tactics employed by black American abolitionists such as Douglass.

O'Connell's stance on slavery undoubtedly led to dissension among American support groups for Repeal, especially but not only in the south. In particular, his 'Great Irish Address', a petition signed by 60,000 Irish people urging Irish Americans to support abolition (December 1841), failed to woo Irish Americans to the abolitionist cause but did drive some from support for Repeal. His abolitionism was also one of a number of bones of contention with the Young Irelanders. While purporting to be anti-slavery, the Young Irelanders opposed O'Connell for his abolitionist stance. As an editorial in their paper *The Nation* stated in April 1845:

> Notwithstanding the slavery of the negro, America is liberty's bulwark and Ireland's dearest ally ... Ireland knows that she has no Quixotic mission to hunt out and quarrel for (without being able to address) distant wrongs, when her own sufferings and thraldom require every exertion and every alliance (O'Connell, 1990: 124).

They elaborated on the final point in a later editorial in February 1847.

> ... we have really so very urgent affairs at home – so much abolition of white slavery to effect if we can... that all our exertions will be needed in Ireland. Carolina

planters never devoured our substance, nor drove away
our sheep and oxen for a spoil ... Our enemies are nearer
home than Carolina ... (*ibid*: 126).

Frederick Douglass' views on the Young Irelanders mirror
those of his hero O'Connell. In later years he bewailed
O'Connell's death because 'the cause of the American slave, not
less than the cause of his country, had met with a great loss'.
Moreover, O'Connell 'was succeeded by the Duffys, Mitchells
(sic), Meaghers, and others, men who loved liberty for
themselves and their country but were utterly destitute of
sympathy with the cause of liberty in countries other than their
own' (Douglass, 1962: 238).[40]

Douglass idolised Daniel O'Connell. He went to visit
Kilmainham Jail to see for himself where O'Connell had been
imprisoned (*ibid*: 123) and attended a huge repeal meeting in
Dublin's Conciliation Hall to hear O'Connell speak. 'I have
heard many speakers within the last four years – speakers of the
first order; but I confess, I have never heard one by whom I was
more completely captivated than by Mr O'Connell' (Foner,
1975a: 121). That evening, O'Connell introduced Douglass to
the large audience as 'the Black O'Connell of the United States'
(Douglass, 1962: 237).

Respect for O'Connell was shared by other black
abolitionists. For example, Robert Purvis, co-founder of the
American Anti-Slavery Society, was introduced to O'Connell
at the House of Commons in 1836. Purvis was light-
complexioned and O'Connell mistook him for a white
American, refusing to shake his hand initially. When he was
told who Purvis was, he pointed out that he never shook the
hand of an American without first ascertaining where the
person stood on the issue of slavery (Fryer, 1984: 432). Thirty
years later, in a speech in New York to commemorate three
decades of the American Anti-Slavery Society, Purvis
recounted his meeting and suggested a variation on
O'Connell's test – that one should ascertain where an

Englishman or Irishman stood on slavery before shaking his hand. 'O'Connell has gone, and, alas! his spirit with him. The foulest and bitterest enemies of freedom and the black man are countrymen of the great Liberator' (Foner and Brahnam, 1998: 395).

In Dublin, surrounded by Webb's company of 'anti-everythingarians', Douglass gravitated for a time towards the temperance movement and its founder Father Theobald Mathew. On 31 August 1845 he gave his first Irish lecture in Celbridge, County Kildare on the evils of alcohol (McFeely, 1991: 124).[41] In a letter to William Lloyd Garrison four months later he stated that, 'The immediate, and it may be the main cause of the extreme poverty and beggary in Ireland, is intemperance' (Foner, 1975a: 141).

He was, however, a much more aware observer and astute commentator on social and political events than such statements might at first reveal. For example, he was well aware of the fact that the Famine was occurring in Ireland and was able to identify with its victims. He wrote to Garrison of visiting a mud-walled and windowless hut, of garbage and filth: 'I see much here to remind me of my former condition and I confess I should be ashamed to lift my voice against American slavery, but that I know the cause of humanity is one the world over' (McFeely, 1991: 126). Although aware of the need not to openly criticise his hosts, he was clear in his writings of the grave injustices experienced by the Irish: 'They have been long oppressed; and the same heart that prompts me to plead the cause of the American bondsmen, makes it impossible not to sympathise with the oppressed of all lands' (quoted in Aptheker, 1969: 312).

Douglass was enraptured by his reception in Ireland, not least by the absence of prejudice on account of the colour of his skin. He wrote to Garrison on 16 September 1845:

> I go on stage coaches, omnibuses, steamboats, into the first cabins, and in the first public houses, without seeing the slightest manifestation of that hateful and vulgar

feeling against me. I find myself not treated as a colour, but as a man – not as a thing, but as a child of the common Father of us all (*ibid*: 120).

Three months later, he was even more effusive.

Instead of a democratic government, I am under a monarchical government. Instead of the bright blue sky of America, I am covered with the soft grey fog of the Emerald Isle, I breathe, and lo! The chattel becomes a man. I gaze around in vain for one who will question my equal humanity, claim me as his slave, or offer me an insult. I employ a cab – I am shown into the same parlor – I dine at the same table – and no one is offended. No delicate nose grows deformed in my presence (*ibid*: 127).

In December 1845 Douglass came to Belfast to give seven lectures. He was immediately struck by the potential to get his abolitionist message across in the city. He wrote to Richard Davis Webb on 6 December: 'The field here is ripe for the harvest; this is the very hotbed of presbyterianism and free churchism, a blow can be struck here more effectually than in any other part of Ireland' (Foner 1975b: 13). What he was referring to became clear on the fifth of his Belfast lectures, given under the auspices of the Belfast Anti-Slavery Committee, and chaired by James Standfield, on 23 December 1845. Douglass had realised that the deeply religious abolitionists of Belfast could be rallied by the accusation of hypocrisy against slave owners who professed to be Christian. Among other examples he singled out, in a speech lasting more than two hours, the case of the Free Church of Scotland, led by Rev. Thomas Chalmers. Chalmers had set out on an ambitious missionary endeavour to convert the urban poor of Scotland, but needed money for his crusade. So members of his Free Church went to America on a fund-raising tour. They had little success in the north, but in the slaveholding south were particularly successful. They returned to Scotland with £3,000, most of it raised in South Carolina (McFeely, 1991: 129). Chalmers had been criticised over accepting money from slave-owners in a pamphlet published by the Belfast Anti-Slavery Committee. And so Douglass was speaking to a knowledgeable and sympathetic audience when he focused on the hypocrisy of people like the Rev. Thomas Chalmers.

> My motto is, 'No union with the slave-holder'. (Cheers) Because, I believe there can be no union between light and darkness... I may be told, 'judge not, that ye be not judged?' I admit the truth of this part of Scripture, but those who read it to me should read a little further, where it is said, 'by their fruits ye shall know them'. (Cheers) I do not judge you when you cut me, if I cry out that you hurt me. (Hear) It is not judging the state of your soul, when I tell you that you have done me an injury. I know that, by injuring me, you are acting contrary to Christianity, and when you tell me that there are some Christian slave-holders in the States, I tell you as well may you talk of sober-drunkards. (Laughter) ... there is no greater calamity than being the slave of a Christian slave-holder. (Hear) ... A man becomes the more cruel the more the religious element is perverted in him ... if they are women-whippers, cradle-plunderers, and man-stealers before their conversion, they are women-whippers, cradle-plunderers, and man stealers after it – (hear) – and that 'religion' is to them but an additional stimulant to re-enact their atrocious deeds' (*Belfast Newsletter*, 26 December 1845).

Echoing O'Connell's campaign, he went on to urge the audience to 'send back the money', and this became his rallying cry at meetings from that point on.

Before he had arrived in Ulster, letters to the *Banner of Ulster*, a local paper, had questioned Douglass' sincerity and suggested that he was an imposter. His only other negative experience during his four months and 50 lectures in Ireland was in Waterford, where people were a little wary of him because they remembered a previous occasion when Moses Roper, another black abolitionist, had turned up drunk to give a lecture (Rice,

1981: 132).[42] But he need not have worried. His audience that night responded rapturously to his oratory. 'That night in Belfast, Frederick Douglass had achieved one of the greatest emotional triumphs of his life' (McFeely, 1991: 130).

After Belfast, Douglass moved on to Scotland to push home his message and spoke in halls decorated with posters saying: 'Send back the money' (Foner, 1975a: 65).[43] And in retaliation, Free Church of Scotland members paraded in Belfast carrying placards saying, 'Send back the nigger' (Rice, 1981: 132). Despite countless mass meetings, especially in Scotland, the money was never returned.[44]

Moses Roper

7. Legacy

B y the 20th century, the patterns of Irish encounters with and attitudes towards people of colour were long-established – on the one hand positive internationalism, on the other, racism. The 20th century brought many more opportunities for such encounters, which were then easily assimilated into the already existing patterns.

The Republic of Ireland and the United Nations

The partition of Ireland in 1921 created two inward-looking states. But as the century progressed, the outside world began to penetrate the two cocooned societies. In the South, membership of the United Nations in 1955 proved to be a change with long-lasting consequences. Because of its colonial past, Ireland was quickly seen by other colonial and ex-colonial states as an ally. It confirmed this perception by taking a line at times at odds with the wishes of the major powers in the UN. Within two years of its accession, it had agreed to support a vote for the admission of China to the body, much to the annoyance of the US. The fact that the Republic of Ireland had arrived on the world stage was brought home to its citizens by events in the 1960s as a result of its involvement in UN activity relating to a number of conflicts resulting from the decolonisation of Africa. In July 1960, the province of Katanga seceded from the Congo. In the war that followed, Irish personnel played a key role. Irish troops were sent in a peace-keeping capacity (only the second time they had been thus deployed, the first being in Lebanon in 1957). And an Irish diplomat, Conor Cruise O'Brien, came to international prominence because of his country's capable handling of affairs; he later went on to become Minister for Posts and Telegraphs in a coalition government in the Republic (O'Brien, 1962).

Africa loomed again in public consciousness later in the decade. In 1967, the province of Biafra broke away from the recently decolonised federal state of Nigeria and a three year war ensued. Federal troops finally overthrew the breakaway government and armed forces, but not before famine devastated Biafra. In the days long before Live Aid and Comic Relief, the plight of Biafra touched international opinion, nowhere more so than in Ireland. Nigeria was the 'jewel in the crown' (Staunton, 2000: 44) of the Irish religious missions overseas; Irish missionaries taught more children and cared for more sick in Nigeria than in the rest of African countries combined. The Independent newspaper group in Dublin spearheaded an appeal which raised £278,000 by 1969, and government and other sources provided at least the same again (*ibid*: 46). Irish Catholic missionaries circumvented a Nigerian blockade of Biafra by airlifting supplies, journalists and photographers from neighbouring countries, angering the Nigerian authorities who accused them of also running guns to the secessionists. Impressive as the support undoubtedly was, to a population raised on donating money to 'the black babies' the humanitarian effort on behalf of Biafra did nothing to shatter racist stereotypes about the dependency of Africa and its inhabitants.

Northern Ireland and World War II

In the North, the first major encounter with the outside world after partition resulted from the Second World War. American troops gathered in the North in 1942 in preparation for the D-Day landings in France. There were 120,000 troops in all, 'several thousand' of whom were black (Dooley, 1998: 24). Overall, they seem to have been relatively well received by the civilian population. There was no evidence that nationalists took a cue from the neutrality of the government in the South to boycott the American soldiers, white or black. In fact, one unionist MP in County Derry complained that the women going out with the black GIs were 'mostly of the lowest type and belong to our minority' (Barton, 1995: 103). In reality, the black soldiers had most to fear from their fellow (white) Americans; fights were common and one black soldier was killed by white American troops in Antrim (Dooley, 1998: 24). Their treatment at the hands of British troops stationed in the North seems to have been little better. For a while, the social relations of the deep South of the US were recreated in Northern Ireland. Segregation, imposed by the US military authorities, became commonplace. In Magherafelt, for example, white and black troops were required to frequent the bars on alternate nights. Elsewhere mixing in pubs, dance halls and parties off-base was actively discouraged. At least some of the locals seem to have taken to the discourse of southern whites like ducks to water. One black soldier based in Antrim wrote anonymously to the Northern Ireland government.

> … a friend and I visited Hall's [a hotel in Antrim], they refused to serve us because we are colored … We hate to walk the streets of Belfast because we are insulted. They use the words 'nigger' and 'darky'. Those are two words that we hate. Those words were brought here by the American whites. (Barton, 1995: 103-4)

Civil rights

After the war, the black soldiers went back to being second class citizens in America while the northern nationalists continued as second class citizens in their own state. In time, both groups began agitation for civil rights. The parallels between developments in both campaigns during the 1960s are remarkable, not least because Irish nationalists were aware, as a result of television, of the plight of black Americans. During the first civil rights protest in Dungannon in 1963 one placard read: 'Racial discrimination in Alabama hits Dungannon' (Dooley, 1998: 30). A century after black-face minstrels were the rage in Ireland, a young boy on a protest march in Dungannon in 1963 blackened his face and carried a sign referring to the similarities between Alabama and the North (*ibid*: 31). In addition, civil rights activists in the North consciously modelled elements of their campaign on what black Americans were doing contemporaneously. People's Democracy (PD), the radical political grouping formed by students in 1968, was influenced by the American Student Non-Violent Coordinating Committee. PD's leading activist, Michael Farrell, took the precedent of Martin Luther King's march from Selma to Montgomery in 1965 as the prototype for the long march from Belfast to Derry in January 1969 (*ibid*: 4). And there were direct contacts between PD and black activists in the US. PD's Eilis McDermott visited Boston in November 1969 and met with the Black Panthers (*ibid*: 53). Bernadette Devlin, the young civil rights MP, visited on two occasions during the period – August 1969 and February 1971. On the first occasion, she was symbolically presented with the keys to the city by New York City mayor John Lindsay; she immediately gave them to another leading civil rights activist, Eamonn McCann, who passed them on to the Black Panthers (Devlin, 1988: 87).45 In 1971, she caused a stir by visiting Angela Davis, the black radical in jail awaiting trial for murder and kidnapping (Dooley, 1998: 66). Nor was the traffic solely one-way: three members of Martin Luther King's Southern Christian Leadership Conference, including Juanita Abernethy, attended a Northern Ireland Civil Rights Association meeting in Belfast two weeks after the Bloody Sunday massacre in January 1972 (*ibid*: 67).

Racism in Ireland

Thirty years on, Ireland was a very changed place. In the South the 'Celtic tiger' phenomenon changed many aspects of society which people had come to believe were endemic. The economy boomed on the back of international investment, unemployment fell rapidly and emigration ceased. By the end of the century, the Republic of Ireland was experiencing net immigration. Included in those arriving were refugees from Eastern Europe and the Balkans as well as Nigerians, the latter partly influenced by Ireland's long-established and positive links to that country through missionary activity. It was a case of the religious empire coming home to roost. But unlike in the 1960s, there was often little sign of empathy. Racial hostility and attacks became commonplace (Cullen, 2000; Harris and Byrne, 2001). Despite relatively low numbers of migrants, a moral panic ensued, paradoxically aided and abetted by the same newspaper chain that had been so instrumental in bringing the plight of Biafrans to public consciousness (Pollak, 1999).

In the North, the immigrants who arrived in the last quarter of the century were from within the British Empire. The first Chinese arrived from the New Territories of Hong Kong in the early 1960s, increasing in the 1970s and afterwards so that by the end of the century they had become the largest ethnic minority group (with about 7000 members; Watson and McKnight, 1998). In the 1960s and 1970s, large numbers of Indians migrated to Britain, some of whom then moved on to Northern Ireland. By 1995, there were around 1000 resident (Kapur, 1997; Irwin, 1998). Likewise Pakistani Muslims arrived from Britain in the same period, with about 600-700 resident by the end of the century (Donnan and O'Brien, 1998).[46] In time these ethnic minority groups were joined by a trickle of refugees from the Balkans and Eastern Europe. As in the South, racist hostility became commonplace (Connolly and Keenan, 2000) and racial attacks occurred.

To the casual observer, either within or outside Ireland, the rise of racism North and South appeared not only unexpected but also somehow unnatural; this was, after all, 'Ireland of the welcomes'. Yet the racism did not come out of nowhere. For centuries, the Irish had been encountering people of colour at home and abroad, often in situations where the Irish were part of the forces colonising or subjugating the people of colour. Those people of colour who arrived in Ireland were often powerless also, marginalised as slaves, entertainers or 'freaks'. The Irish had countless opportunities throughout history to be reminded of their relative superiority and while that lesson may have lain dormant at various times, it only needed the excuse of immigration to be awakened.

But, as we have argued here, there is also another history – one of mutual respect between Irish and black people – which produced such key figures as Daniel O'Connell and Frederick Douglass. For those who wish to follow in their footsteps, it is crucial to confront the history of the past, to know the roots of racism and also the ferment of anti-racism, and thereby to reject the former and nurture the latter.

Notes

1. In reply to the claim of the Chinese Welfare Association that Chinese people were being increasingly targeted, he stated: 'Short of asking the perpetrators, I don't know how they know these attacks are racist'. (*Belfast Telegraph*, 20 November 2000).
2. For a comprehensive account of racism and anti-racism in contemporary Ireland, see Lentin and McVeigh, 2002.
3. Waterford's familiarity with slave trading is evidenced in the popular song of the early 19th century, 'William Hollander'. It tells the story of a young man from the county who enlists on a slaving ship running slaves from Africa to Cuba. He later becomes a pirate in the Caribbean and is captured and sentenced to hang at Newgate Prison. The moral of the song, emphasised in the last verse, is this: 'So come all young men a warning take and shun all piracy'. Surprisingly, the sentiments of the song are not brutal; Hollander clearly empathises with the slaves. When half of them die on a voyage and their bodies are thrown overboard, he says: 'Far better for the rest of them if they had died below/ Than beneath the planters' bully boys all on the Cuban shore'. (For a version of the song, see Robbie O'Connell, 'Close to the Bone', Green Linnet Records, 1982.)
4. The colonial merchants in the British West Indies found themselves on the horns of a dilemma as regards Irish indentured servants. On the one hand, the Irish, because of poverty, were among the most eager to immigrate; on the other hand they were 'a riotous and unruly lot' who harboured Jacobin thoughts and were not averse to joining in slave rebellions from time to time. For example, in 1666, the Irish servants and freemen on St. Kitts celebrated the announcement of war between England and France by rising up against the English and aiding the French to take control of the island, evicting 800 English planters in the process. The following year, the Irish on Montserrat also helped the French to take the island from the English. In 1689, when word reached the Caribbean of William of Orange's accession to the English throne, the Irish again revolted on St. Kitts and plundered English estates in support of the ousted King James. The same happened on St. Christopher, and Antigua and Montserrat were on the edge of mutiny. No wonder that one leading St. Kitts planter, Christopher Jeaffreson, wrote in 1673: 'Scotchmen and Welshmen we esteem the best servants, and the Irish the worst, many of them being good for nothing but mischief' (quoted in Beckles, 1992: 511)

5. Nash (1985: 335) notes the different diets of slaves and owners, thus revealing that while each was dependent on provisioning from abroad, the white population was more dependent than the black. 'A British owner typically supplied his slaves with a pint or two of corn per day and a pound of cod per week. The slaves eked out these provisions with poultry and vegetables raised on their own plots and with the goods for which they traded these products in the ubiquitous Sunday markets. In contrast, white indentured servants received plenty of salted meat, while the free white population consumed ample quantities of provisions as well as more palatable foodstuffs.'

6. The impoverished sitting tenants, facing the prospect of eviction, fought back by maiming Greg's cattle. As a result, one man was arrested in December 1770 and imprisoned in Belfast. Over 1000 members of the agrarian society, the Hearts of Steel, attacked the barracks where he was held and succeeded in freeing the prisoner, but not before the military had shot dead five of their number and injured many others. In retaliation, they fired shots into Thomas Greg's house and set fire to Waddell Cunningham's home in Hercules Lane.

7. Links with Africa may be even older. Wagner (1982) claims that the 'substratum' of insular Celtic, including Gaelic, reveals patterns which show its relationship to Egyptian and Berber, two Hamitic languages of North Africa. This is a minority view within Celtic Studies which is easily misrepresented – as, for example, in the *Irish Times*' (28 May, 2000) heading 'North Africans may have beaten Celts to Ireland' in an otherwise sober article on the work of the attempts of the Department of Linguistics of the Max Planck Institute for Evolutionary Anthropology, following Wagner's lead, to map the origins of Gaelic (see http://www.eva.mpg.de/lingua.html).

8. North African influence is perhaps also evident in the Tau, or Coptic cross, sometimes carved on stone crosses (see illustration of one carving at Broughanlee, County Antrim, in Marshall, 1987). In addition, there is a plausible argument that the instantly recognisable Celtic cross which flourished in Ireland in the ninth century was modelled directly on the earlier Coptic cross, itself possibly deriving from the Egyptian *ankh* which had been central in Egyptian iconography for a millennium before Coptic Christianity emerged (see Horn et al., 1990: 89-96)

9. 'Slaves, though not generally available on a large scale, were important ... and probably supplied a lot of the domestic labour in the homes of the elite ...' (Patterson, 1994: 152).

10. The first reliable record of a visit by Jewish ambassadors to Ireland is given in the *Annals of Innisfallen* for the year 1079; five Jews,

probably from Rouen, came with gifts to the court of Tairdelbach Ua Briain; see MacAirt, 1951: 233.

11. Crusaders who had made it to the Holy Land often took new names such as Jordan and Palmer, surnames which can be found in contemporary Ireland.

12. The incident was immortalised in song two centuries later by the Young Irelander, Thomas Davis. 'And o'er each black and bearded face,/ The white or crimson shawl –/ The yell of 'Allah' breaks above,/ The pray'r and shriek, and roar –/ O blessed God! The Algerine/ Is lord of Baltimore' (Healey, 1967: 48-50).

13. Another Hibernian Regiment soldier, Viscount Arthur Magennis, was captured in the 1730s and enslaved for four years. His kinsman, Eneas Mac Donnell, another one of the 'wild geese', suffered a similar but briefer fate when captured by corsairs in 1683 (see McDonnell, 1996: 54 and 146).

14. Some tantalising possible evidence of the presence of black soldiers at the Boyne is the fact that the reputedly oldest public house in Ireland dates from 1736 and was known as 'The Three Blackamoors Head' (later 'The Three Blacks Inn'). The pub is in Athlone which was the gateway for the Williamite army as it conquered the west at the Battle of Aughrim and later Limerick. (see Murtagh, 2000)

15. An encounter of a very different kind between black Americans and Irish soldiers in the British Army occurred around the same time. A black American, Prince Hall, attempted to join the Masonic Lodge in Boston but was refused by the white Masons there. He then approached the military lodge of an Irish Regiment of the British Army under the command of General Gage – Lodge 441. On 6 March 1775, Hall and 15 other black men were initiated as Masons and eleven days later the regiment was forced to evacuate Boston as hostilities increased. Hall retitled the Lodge African Lodge No. 1. It was 1787 before the Lodge was fully incorporated. See Foner, 1975c: 559-560.

16. Canny (1998: 161) mentions the intriguing case of an unhappy encounter between native Americans and Irish, this time in Ireland itself. John Fortune was a native American who seemingly came to Europe and may well have fought in the Thirty Years War. He ended up in Ireland where he 'had the misfortune to be mistaken for an English Protestant by Irish Catholic insurgents in the rising of 1641'.

17. For a time the legal demarcation between slavery and servitude was not particularly clear. Thus planters frequently encouraged sexual relations between white (often Irish) women servants and male black slaves in the hope of thereby enslaving their offspring. In 1681 one such liaison was considered by the courts in Maryland and the servant, known only as Irish Nell, and her black partner succeeded in having their children declared free rather than slaves. Thereafter laws

throughout the South specified that such children would be kept as servants for a set period of time, often until they were aged 30 (Woodson and Wesley, 1970: 111-2).

18. There were a number of factors which ensured that the Irish ended up more racist than other established European immigrant groups. 'Economically more secure than the Irish, other immigrant groups had little fear of Negro competition and generally adopted a more tolerant racial outlook' (Litwack, 1961: 166).

19. The victory of the Irish worker over the Afro-American was later underwritten by claims of management theorists, in effect rubbing salt in the wounds. Thus, in an article entitled 'Negroes as a Source of Industrial Labor' written in 1918, D.T. Farnham argued that 'because of their "type" … Irish foremen are deemed the best bosses of Negro labor. Firmness is absolutely necessary with them' (Johnson, 1958: 75).

20. There is also evidence of inter-marriage. Thus famous black Americans such as Muhammed Ali, Alice Walker, Billie Holiday (born Eleonara Gough Fagan), Ella Fitzgerald and Alex Haley could point to Irish as well as African roots (see Daniel Cassidy, 'Churches of fire in Ireland and the South', *San Francisco Chronicle*, 29 July 1998).

21. At a cultural level too, Ireland proved to be a beacon to some Afro-Americans. Writing in 1921, James Weldon Johnson, later a leading figure in the Harlem Renaissance, stated: 'What a colored poet in the United States needs to do is something like what Synge did for the Irish; he needs to find a form that will express the racial spirit by symbols from within rather than by symbols from without, such as the mere mutilation of English spelling and pronunciation' (Levy, 1973: 304). Harry Belafonte has acknowledged the influence of Sean O'Casey on his development, and James Baldwin that of James Joyce on his (see Dooley, 1998: 5-6).

22. On hearing the news of Mac Swiney's death on hunger strike, Ho Chi Minh, then working as a dishwasher in a London hotel, stated: 'A nation which has such citizens will never surrender' (Ellis, 1985: 254). Over four decades later he was leading the Vietnamese in a war against American imperialism.

23. Griffith had spent two years as a journalist in South Africa (from 1896 to 1898) where, like his fellow expatriate John McBride, he had clearly sided with the Boers against the English. Despite the comments on John Mitchel cited, his attitudes to the local black population seem to have been more patronizing than aggressively racist. He was even capable of recognizing the plight of the indigenous population, albeit as a means of criticizing the English. The English, he said, 'told the black man he was a man and a brother and then treated him like a dog' (McCracken, 1996: 253).

24. The racism was not confined to convicts. In 1857, Michael Normile, an Irish immigrant to Australia, wrote to his father in Ireland displaying a subtle hierarchy of racism. 'I mean to inform you about the native Blacks of this Coloney. They are an ugly race of people they go about in numbers from one place to another. They have a King for every tribe or district. He wears a badge of honour a pice of Brass with his name engraved on it... As for the American Blacks they are of a nice complection and very good worksmen & all of them roman Catholicks & very industrious' (Fitzpatrick, 1994: 78).

25. Miller (1985) uses letters from Irish Catholic immigrants in America for his monumental account of emigration. However, there is little direct reference in these letters to encounters with black Americans.

26. Irish involvement in slave trading was not confined to England. Nantes was the leading port in the French slave trade. An instigator of the first slave trade company there, Société d'Angole, formed in September 1748, was Antoine Walsh, a second-generation Irish immigrant. He later went on to form the first private joint stock slave trade company in France, with generous backing from the banks (Stein, 1979: 280).

27. The original is in the National Portrait Gallery in London. Randell Mac Donnell was probably not the only member of his clan to have a slave. In fact, given the English fashion of the time for the rich to own black slaves, it was one of the ways in which the clan could prove its loyalty by showing how English and up-to-date they were. In this vein, two paintings in the possession of Lord O'Neill at Shane's Castle, Randalstown, County Antrim are of interest. They show Rose, second wife of the Marquis of Antrim in the mid-17th century, with her black slave. There is also a portrait of Rose's father Henry, also accompanied by a black slave (see page 55).

28. Referring to media coverage of Casement's arrest and execution for his involvement in the 1916 Rising, Moses (1978: 224) notes: 'So fully committed to the war effort and the struggle with Germany were his majesty's Negro subjects, that Casement's well-known sympathies for the African peoples did not prevent his being roundly denounced. West Africans seemed to be completely blind to any similarities that may have existed between their own nationalistic aspirations and the Irish struggle for independence from England.'

29. It is interesting to note that the Easter Rising involved around 1000 Irish insurgents and was put down by approximately 2,500 British troops, the bulk of whom were Irish (Karsten, 1983: 47).

30. Engels proceeds in his very next sentence to reveal his highly racialised view of the Irish: 'The Irishman is a carefree, cheerful, potato-eating child of nature'. So, why would any such person want to overthrow an empire? 'The half-savage upbringing and later the completely civilised environment bring the Irishman into

contradiction with himself, into a state of permanent irritation, of continually smouldering fury, which makes him capable of anything'. Almost as an afterthought, he adds to this sociopathic explanation: 'In addition, he bears the burden of five centuries of oppression...' (Marx and Engels, 1979: 43).

31. The Orange Order has lodges wherever emigration brought previous waves of northern Protestant emigrants – the United States, Canada, Australia, New Zealand. Most of the members of lodges in these countries are descendants of the original emigrants, but there are some lodges composed of descendants of the colonized, most notably, the Mohawk nation in Canada, and black Orangemen in Ghana. It would appear that where political and indeed sectarian ideology and conflict were often central to the white Orangemen, especially in the United States and Australia, it was the religious content which attracted the Orangemen of a different colour. (See Kennedy, 1990: 82-96 for photographs of Mohawk and Ghanaian Orangmen.)

32. The Irish Protestant churches also had their missionaries, but fewer than the Catholics. In 1996, for example, there were 2294 Catholic missionaries in Africa compared to 85 Protestants (Church of Ireland, Methodist and Presbyterian; see Coogan, 2000: 504). For historical details of Irish Catholic and Protestant missionary activity in India, see Kapur, 1997: 7-14.

33. The nine year old Frank McCourt was also confronted with a bizarre collection device which was common at the time when his dance teacher brought him a tin in the form of 'a black boy with kinky hair, big eyes, huge red lips and an open mouth'. The money was to be placed in the mouth. (On McCourt's treatment of Africa and Africans, see El-Tom, 1998.) Another writer, Mary Lavin, recounts her own childhood mistake; told that if she brought in enough 'black baby money' in school, she would get to name an African baby, she seriously concluded that an actual baby was going to be sent to her afterwards.

34. Interestingly, despite the early involvement of Belfast in overseas trade, including with the Caribbean, there is no evidence in recent history of black sailors having settled in the port (according to Pat Benson, chair of Sailortown Resident's Association, personal communication).

35. She has not been forgotten in the new South Africa. See the poem 'For Sara Baartman' by Diane Ferrus, in *Words in the House of Sound* (2000). 'I have come to wrench you away/ away from the poking eyes/ ... I have come to take you home –/ where the ancient mountains shout your name'.

36. As the story shows, it was common in Britain and Ireland to give slaves classical names such as Caesar, Hector and Dido. In an

interesting reversal of this trend, slaves on the island of Montserrat, which had originally contained many Irish indentured servants, were called by the names of Irish counties such as 'Dublin' and 'Kilkenny' (see McDowell, 1974: 51).

37. As Douglass' star waxed, Remond's waned. 'When the country … had heard Frederick Douglass, Remond become a second-rate man. This soured the spirit of the latter; and he fell a victim to speaking disparagingly of his co-worker' (Woodson and Wesley, 1970: 315).

38. The following day, the Rev. Robert Templeton, pastor of the Presbyterian church in Hillsborough, County Down, wrote to the *Belfast Newsletter* to complain that Allen had been scheduled to speak in Hillsborough, but chose to go to Downpatrick instead. Allen wrote a reply to the same newspaper. 'I called upon Mr Templeton on Saturday afternoon last, and stated the object of my visit, which was, as he rightly describes, "to secure his aid and influence in procuring a place to deliver, and an audience to hear, a lecture which I designed to give in Hillsborough". He dissuaded me, sure enough, and drew such a gloomy picture of the lecture-going tendencies of the inhabitants of Hillsborough as would have discouraged any man not "bent", as Mr Templeton adds, "on making the experiment"' (Ripley: 1985: 424).

39. He was, said the great American abolitionist William Lloyd Garrison, 'incomparably more than a mere geographical Irishman' (Riach, 1980: 185).

40. In 1855 the paths of Douglass and the Young Irelanders crossed again. Thomas Meagher, a leading Young Irelander, had been transported to Van Diemen's Land for his role in the 1848 rebellion in Ireland. Later he arrived in the United States where he was given permission by a special order of the Supreme Court to practice law despite not having taken any American examinations. Douglass objected that the native born black American, unlike Meagher, received no such privileges as a matter of courtesy. (Foner 1975c: 365) Later Meagher, in his newspaper, the *Irish News*, went on, like John Mitchel, to support slavery.

41. A high point of his visit is when he made his pledge – his promise to abstain from alcohol – to Father Mathew personally and was delighted to announce in a letter to the American abolitionist William Lloyd Garrison in October 1845 that he was the 5,487,395th person to do so (Foner, 1975b: 9). Garrison himself visited Ireland in July 1870 in the company of Charles Lenox Remond. He gave some abolitionist lectures, including one in Belfast which created 'no small stir' (Merrill, 1963: 195).

42. Roper's autobiography (1970) was published originally in 1838 and therefore gives no information about his trip to Ireland three years later .

43. Douglass continued to be politically involved on the Irish issue up to his death in 1895. He appeared on platforms with Charles Stewart Parnell and supported Home Rule (Dooley, 1998: 17). He visited Ireland again briefly in September 1886. But he found that the people he had been so well received by on his first visit – such as Richard Davis Webb in Dublin and the Workman family in Belfast, and others – 'were now all gone, and except some of their children, I was among strangers' (Douglass, 1962: 560).
44. The campaign, incidentally, caused some embarrassment to Irish abolitionists as money had been sent from Southern U.S. states for famine relief in Ireland (Temperley, 1972: 218).
45. 'I was not very long there until, like water, I found my own level. "My people" – the people who knew about oppression, discrimination, prejudice, poverty and the frustration and despair that they produce – were not Irish-Americans. They were black, Puerto Rican, chicano. And those who were supposed to be "my people" ... said exactly the same things about blacks that the loyalists said about us at home' (Devlin, 1988: 87).
46. By way of comparison: there were 70 Jews in the North of Ireland in 1871, about the time the first synagogue was built in Belfast. In 1965, that number had grown to around 1500, but by 1997 had reduced drastically to 230; Warm, 1998.

Bibliography

Agnew, Jean. *Belfast Merchant Families in the 17ᵗʰ Century*, Dublin, Four Courts Press, 1996

Agnew, Jean (ed). *The Drennan-McTier Letters, volume 3, 1802-1819*, Dublin, Women's History Project, in association with Irish Manuscripts Commission, 1999

Aptheker, Herbert (ed). *A Documentary History of the Negro People in the United States*, New York, Citadel Press, 1969.

Bartlett, Thomas (ed). *Life of Theobald Wolfe Tone*, Dublin, Lilliput Press, 1998

Barton, Brian. *Northern Ireland in the Second World War*, Belfast, Ulster Historical Foundation, 1995

Beckles, Hilary. 'A "Riotous and Unruly Lot": Irish Indentured Servants and Freemen in the English West Indies 1644-1713', *William and Mary Quarterly*, 47, 1990: 503-522

Cahill, Thomas. *How the Irish Saved Civilization*, New York, Doubleday, 1995

Canny, Nicholas. 'England's New World and the Old, 1480s-1630s', in N. Canny (ed). *The Origins of Empire: British Overseas Enterprise to the Close of the Seventeenth Century*, Oxford University Press, 1998: 148-169

Chambers, George. *Faces of Change: the Belfast and Northern Ireland Chambers of Commerce and Industry 1783-1983*, Belfast, Northern Ireland Chamber of Commerce and Industry, 1983

Clarke, H.B. 'The Bloodied Eagle: the Vikings and the Development of Dublin, 841-1014', *The Irish Sword* XVIII (70), 1990: 91-119

Connolly, Paul and Keenan, Michaela. *Racial attitudes and prejudice in Northern Ireland*, Belfast, Northern Ireland Statistics and Research Agency, 2000

Coogan, Tim Pat. *Wherever Green is Worn: the Story of the Irish Diaspora*, , London, Hutchinson, 2000

Cooper, Wayne F. *Claude McKay: Rebel Sojourner in the Harlem Renaissance*, Baton Rouge and London, Louisiana State University Press, 1987

Costelloe, Con. *Ireland and the Holy Land: an Account of Irish Links with the Levant from Earliest Times*, Alcester and Dublin, C. Godliffe Neale, 1974

Crookshank, Anne and The Knight of Glin. *The Painters of Ireland c.1660-1920*, London, Barrie and Jenkins, 1979

Cullen, Paul. *Refugees and Asylum-Seekers in Ireland*, Cork University Press, 2000

Curtin, John. 'A Brave Slave, Robert St. George', *The Old Limerick Journal*, Winter 1999: 30-31

Davis, David Brion. *The Problem of Slavery in the Age of Revolution, 1770-1823*, Ithaca, Cornell University Press, 1975

Devlin, Bernadette. 'A Peasant in the Halls of the Great', in Michael Farrell (ed). *Twenty Years On*, Dingle, Brandon, 1988: 75-88

Doherty, Charles. 'Exchange and Trade in Early Medieval Ireland', *Journal of the Royal Society of Antiquaries of Ireland*, 110, 1980: 67-89

Donnan, Hastings and O'Brien, Mairead. 'Because you stick out, you stand out': Perceptions of prejudice among Northern Ireland's Pakistanis', in Paul Hainsworth (ed). *Divided Society: Ethnic Minorities and Racism in Northern Ireland*, London, Pluto Press, 1998: 197-221

Dooley, Brian. *Black and Green: the Fight for Civil Rights in Northern Ireland and Black America*, London, Pluto Press, 1998

Dooley, Tom. 'The Royal Munster Fusiliers', *History Ireland*, spring 1998: 33-39

Douglass, Frederick. *Life and Times of Frederick Douglass*, New York, Collier Books, 1962 (originally published 1892)

Douglass, Frederick. *Narrative of the Life of Frederick Douglass, an American Slave*, Cambridge, Massachusetts, The Belknap Press of Harvard University Press, 1971 (originally published 1845)

Doyle, Francis Bernard. 'South Africa', in Patrick J. Corish (ed), *A History of Irish Catholicism, vol. VI*, Dublin, Gill and Macmillan, 1971: 1-27

Drescher, Seymour. *Capitalism and Antislavery: British Mobilization in Comparative Perspective*, London, Macmillan, 1986

Edwards, Paul and Walvin, James. *Black Personalities in the Era of the Slave Trade*, London, Macmillan, 1983

Ellis, Peter Berresford. *The Boyne Water*, London, Hamish Hamilton, 1976

Ellis, Peter Berresford. *A History of the Irish Working Class*, London, Pluto1985

El-Tom, Abdullahi Osman. 'McCourt's *Angela's Ashes* and the Portrait of the Other', *Irish Journal of Anthropology*, 3, 1998: 78-90

Evans, E. Estyn. 'The Scotch-Irish: Their Cultural Adaptation and Heritage in the American Old West', in E.R.R. Green (ed). *Essays in Scotch-Irish History*, London, Routledge and Kegan Paul, 1969: 69-86

Falkiner, C. Litton. *Studies in Irish History and Biography, mainly of the Eighteenth Century*, London, Longman, Green and Co., 1902

Fernbane Parish and its Churches, 1979

Ferguson, Kenneth. 'The Organisation of King William's Army in Ireland, 1989-92', *The Irish Sword* XVIII, 70, 1990: 62-79

Fitzpatrick, David. *Oceans of Consolation: Personal Accounts of Irish Migration to Australia*, Ithaca and London, Cornell University Press, 1994

Fitzpatrick, Rory. *God's Frontiersmen: the Scots-Irish Epic*, London, Weidenfeld and Nicolson, 1989

Foner, Philip S. (ed). *The Life and Writings of Frederick Douglass, volume 1. Early Years, 1817-1849*, New York, International Publishers, 1975 (a)

Foner, Philip S. (ed). *The Life and Writings of Frederick Douglass, volume 5. Supplementary Volume, 1844-1860*, New York, International Publishers, 1975 (b)

Foner, Philip S. *History of Black Americans: from Africa to the Emergence of the Cotton Kingdom*, Westport, Connecticut, Greenwood Press, 1975 (c)

Foner, Philip S. *History of Black Americans: from the Emergence of the Cotton Kingdom to the Eve of the Compromise of 1850*, Westport, Connecticut, Greenwood Press, 1983

Foner, Philip S. and Branham, Robert James (eds). *Lift Every Voice: African American Oratory, 1787-1900*, Tuscaloosa, University of Alabama Press, 1998

Foner, Philip S. and Walker, George E. (eds), *Proceedings of the Black State Conventions, 1840-1865, volume 2*, Philadephia, Temple University Press, 1980

Forbes, Jack D. *Black Africans and Native Americans*, Oxford, Basil Blackwell, 1988

Fraser, T.G. 'Ireland and India', in K. Jeffery (ed). *'An Irish Empire'?*

Aspects of Ireland and the British Empire, Manchester, Manchester University Press, 1996: 77-93

Fryer, Peter. *Staying Power: the History of Black People in Britain*, London, Pluto, 1984

Green, E.R.R. 'Ulster Emigrants' Letters', in E.R.R. Green (ed). *Essays in Scotch-Irish History*, London, Routledge and Kegan Paul, 1969: 87-103

Haliday, Charles. *The Scandinavian Kingdom of Dublin*, Shannon, Irish University Press, 1969 (originally published 1881)

Harris, Paul and Byrne, Nicola. 'Arson, abuse, stone-throwing: Ireland's welcome for refugees', *The Observer*, 19 August 2001: 9

Hart, Bill. 'Africans in 18th Century Ireland', unpublished

Higginbotham, A. Leon. *In the Matter of Color: Race and the American Legal Process*, New York, Oxford University Press, 1978

Hill, Robert A. (ed). *The Marcus Garvey and Universal Negro Improvement Association Papers, vol. 1: 1826-August 1919*, Berkeley, University of California Press, 1983

Horn, Walter, Marshall, Jenny White, and Grellan, D. Rourke, *The Forgotten Hermitage of Skellig Michael*, Berkeley, University of California Press, 1990

Hughes, Robert. *The Fatal Shore*, London, Pan Books, 1987

Hyman, Louis. *The Jews of Ireland: from earliest times to the year 1910*, Shannon, Irish University Press, 1972

Ignatiev, Noel. *How the Irish Became White*, New York, Routledge, 1995

Inglis, Brian. *Roger Casement*, Belfast, Blackstaff Press, 1993

Irwin, Greg. 'The Indian Community in Northern Ireland', in Paul Hainsworth (ed). *Divided Society: Ethnic Minorities and Racism in Northern Ireland*, London, Pluto Press, 1998: 184-196

James, D. 'Two Medieval Arabic Accounts of Ireland', *Journal of the Royal Society of Antiquaries of Ireland*, 108, 1978: 5-9

Jeffery, Keith. 'Introduction', in K. Jeffery (ed). *'An Irish Empire'? Aspects of Ireland and the British Empire*, Manchester, Manchester University Press, 1996a: 1-24

Jeffery, Keith. 'The Irish Military Tradition and the British Empire', in K. Jeffery (ed). *'An Irish Empire'? Aspects of Ireland and the British Empire*, Manchester, Manchester University Press, 1996b: 94-122

Johnson, Charles S. *The Negro in American Civilization*, New York, Henry Holt, 1958 (originally published 1930)

Jones, Maldwyn A. 'Ulster Emigration, 1783-1815', in E.R.R. Green (ed). *Essays in Scotch-Irish History*, London, Routledge and Kegan Paul, 1969:46-68

Jordan, Winthrop D. *White Over Black: American Attitudes toward the Negro, 1550-1812*, New York, W.W. Norton, 1977

Kapur, Narinder. *The Irish Raj: Illustrated Stories about Irish in India and Indians in Ireland*, Antrim, Greystone Press, 1997

Karsten, Peter. 'Irish Soldiers in the British Army, 1792-1922: Suborned or Subordinate?', *Journal of Social History*, XV11, 1983: 31-64

Katzman, David M. *Before the Ghetto: Black Detroit in the Nineteenth Century*, Urbana, University of Illinois Press, 1973

Kennedy, Billy (ed). *A Celebration: 1690-1990 – the Orange Institution*, Belfast, Orange Order, 1990

Kiernan, V.G. *The Lords of Human Kind*, London, Weidenfeld and Nicolson, 1969

Keogh, Dermot. *Jews in Twentieth-Century Ireland*, Cork University Press, 1998

Kruger, H. 'India's Freedom Struggle and Beginnings of Solidarity between National Liberation Movements before World War 1 in Various Countries', in P.M. Joshi and M.A. Nareem (eds). *Studies in the Foreign Relations of India*, Hyderabad, State Archives, Government of Andra Pradesh, 1975: 292-323

Lenihan, Maurice. *Limerick, its History and Antiquities, Ecclesiastical, Civil and Military*, Cork, Mercier Press, 1967 (originally published 1886)

Lentin Ronit and McVeigh Robbie.(eds) *Racism and anti-racism in Ireland*, Belfast, Beyond the Pale Publications, 2002 (forthcoming)

Levine, Lawrence W. *Black Culture and Black Consciousness: Afro-American Folk Thought from Slavery to Freedom*, New York, Oxford University Press, 1977

Levy, Eugene. *James Weldon Johnson: Black Leader, Black Voice*, Chicago, University of Chicago Press, 1973

Lewis, Bernard. *The Muslim Discovery of Europe*, London, Weidenfeld and Nicolson,

Litwack, Leon F. *North of Slavery: the Negro in the Free States, 1790-1860*, University of Chicago Press, 1961

Litwack, Leon F. *Been in the Storm so Long: the Aftermath of Slavery*, New York, Alfred A. Knopf, 1980

Lively, Adam. *Masks: Blackness, Race and the Imagination*, London, Chatto and Windus, 1998

Mac Airt, Seán (ed). *The Annals of Inisfallen*, Dublin, The Dublin Institute for Advanced Studies, 1951

MacLaughlin, Jim. *Travellers and Ireland: Whose Country, Whose History?*, Cork University Press, 1998

Mandela, Nelson. *Long Walk to Freedom*, London, Little, Brown and Company, 1994

Marshall, J.D.C. *Forgotten Places of the North Coast*, Armoy, Clegnagh Publishing, 1987

McCourt, Frank. *Angela's Ashes*, London, HarperCollins, 1996

McCracken, Patricia A. 'Arthur Griffith's South African sabbatical', in Donal P. McCracken (ed). 'Ireland and South Africa in Modern

Times', *South African-Irish Studies*, 3, 1996: 227-262

McDonnell, Hector. *The Wild Geese of the Antrim MacDonnells*, Blackrock, Irish Academic Press, 1996

McDowell, R.B. 'Ireland in the Eighteenth Century British Empire', in J.G. Barry (ed). *Historical Studies 9*, Belfast, Blackstaff Press, 1974: 49-63

McFeely, William S. *Frederick Douglass*, New York, W.W. Norton and Co., 1991

McVeigh, Robbie. 'The Specificity of Irish Racism', *Race and Class*, 33(4) 1992: 31-45

McVeigh, Robbie. '"There's no Racism because there's no Black People here": Racism and Anti-racism in Northern Ireland', in Paul Hainsworth (ed). *Divided Society: Ethnic Minorities and Racism in Northern Ireland*, London, Pluto Press, 1998: 11-32

Merrill,Walter M. *Against the Tide: a Biography of Wm. Lloyd Garrison*, Harvard University Press, 1963

Midgley, Clare. *Women Against Slavery: the British Campaigns, 1780-1870*, London, Routledge, 1992

Miller, John. *The Life and Times of William and Mary*, London, Weidenfeld and Nicolson, 1974

Miller, Kerby. *Emigrants and Exiles: Ireland and the Irish Exodus to North America*, New York, Oxford University Press, 1985

Millin, S. Shannon. *Was Waddell Cunningham, Belfast Merchant, 'A Slave-Ship Projector'? An Historical Inquiry*, Belfast, 1926

Mitchel, John. *Jail Journal*, Dublin, 1913

Moody, T.W. *Davitt and Irish Revolution 1846-82*, Oxford, Clarendon Press, 1981

Moses, Wilson Jeremiah. *The Golden Age of Black Nationalism, 1850-1925*, New York, Oxford University Press, 1978

Murtagh, Harman. 'Irish Soldiers Abroad, 1600-1800', in Thomas Bartlett and Keith Jeffery (eds). *A Military History of Ireland*, Cambridge, Cambridge University Press, 1996: 294: 314

Murtagh, Harman. *Athlone: History and Settlement to 1800*, Old Athlone Society, 2000

Nash, R.C. 'Irish Atlantic Trade in the Seventeenth and Eighteenth Centuries', *William and Mary Quarterly*, XLII, 1985: 329-356

Oakes, James. *The Ruling Race: a History of American Slaveholders*, New York, Vintage Books, 1983

O'Brien, Conor Cruise. *To Katanga and Back*, London, Hutchinson, 1962

O'Brien, George. *The Economic History of Ireland in the 17th Century*, Dublin, Maunsel and Co., 1919

O'Brien, William and Ryan, Desmond (eds). *Devoy's Post Bag*, Dublin, Academy Press, 1979

O'Callaghan, Sean. *To Hell or Barbados: the ethnic cleansing of Ireland*, Dingle, Brandon, 2000

O'Connell, Maurice. *Daniel O'Connell: the Man and his Politics*, Blackrock, Irish Academic Press, 1990

Ó Cróinín, Dáibhí. *Early Medieval Ireland, 400-1200*, London, Longman, 1995

O'Farrell, Patrick. *Letters from Irish Australia 1825-1929*, Sydney/Belfast, New South Wales University Press/Ulster Historical Foundation, 1984

O'Ferrall, Fergus. 'Liberty and Catholic Politics, 1710-1990', in M. O'Connell (ed). *Daniel O'Connell: Political Pioneer*, Dublin, 1991: 35-56

Olmsted, Frederick Law. *The Cotton Kingdom: a Traveller's Observations on Cotton and Slavery in the American Slave States*, New York, Alfred A. Knopf, 1953

Patterson, Nerys. *Cattle Lords and Clansmen: the Social Structure of Early Ireland*, University of Notre Dame Press, 1994

Phillips, Ulrich Bonnell. *American Negro Slavery*, Baton Rouge, Louisiana State University Press, 1966 (originally published 1918)

Pollak, Andy. 'An Invitation to Racism? Irish daily newspaper coverage of the refugee issue', in Damien Kiberd (ed). *Media in Ireland: the Search for Ethical Journalism*, Dublin, Open Air, 1999: 33-46

Radner, Joan Newlon. *Fragmentary Annals of Ireland*, Dublin, Dublin Institute for Advanced Studies, 1978

Reid, Gerard (ed). *Great Irish Voices: Over 400 Years of Irish Oratory*, Dublin, Irish Academic Press, 1999

Riach, Douglas C. 'Blacks and Blackface on the Irish Stage, 1830-60', *Journal of American Studies,* 7(3), 1973: 231-241

Riach, Douglas C. 'Daniel O'Connell and American anti-slavery', *Irish Historical Studies*, XX(77), 1976: 3-25

Riach, Douglas C. 'O'Connell and Slavery', in Donal McCartney (ed). *The World of Daniel O'Connell*, Dublin, Mercier Press, 1980: 175-185

Rice, C. Duncan. *The Scots Abolitionists 1833-1861*, Baton Rouge, Louisiana State University Press, 1981

Ripley, C.P. (ed). *The Black Abolitionist Papers, volume 1, The British Isles 1830-1865*, Chapel Hill, University of North Carolina Press, 1985

Rodgers, Nini. 'Equiano in Belfast: a Study of the Anti-Slavery Ethos in a Northern Town', *Slavery and Abolition,* 18(2), 1997: 73-89

Rodgers, Nini. *Equiano and Anti-Slavery in Eighteenth-Century Belfast*, Belfast, The Belfast Society in association with the Ulster Historical Foundation, 2000

Rodgers, Nini. 'Ireland and the Black Atlantic in the eighteenth century', *Irish Historical Studies*, 32, no., 126, 2000: 174-192

Roper, Moses. *A Narrative of the Adventures and Escape of Moses Roper from American Slavery*, New York, Negro Universities Press,

1970 (originally published 1838)

Shannon, William V. *The American Irish: a Political and Social Portrait*, Amherst, University of Massachusetts Press, 1974

Sheehan, John. 'Early Viking Age Silver Hoards from Ireland', in H.B. Clarke et al., (eds). *Ireland and Scandinavia in the Early Viking Age*, Dublin, Four Courts Press, 1998: 166-202

Silvestri, Michael. 'Sir Charles Tegart and Revolutionary Terrorism in Bengal', *History Ireland*, Winter 2000: 40-44

Staunton, Edna. 'The Forgotten War: the Catholic Church and Biafra (1967-1970)', *History Ireland*, Autumn 2000: 44-48

Stein, Robert Louis. *The French Slave Trade in the 18th Century*, University of Wisconsin Press, 1979

Tattersfield, Nigel. *The Forgotten Trade*, London, Pimlico, 1998

Temperley, Howard. *British Antislavery, 1833-1870*, London, Longman, 1972

Tillyard, Stella. *Citizen Lord: Edward Fitzgerald 1763-1798*, London, Chatto and Windus, 1997

Tomlinson, Mike. 'Imprisoned Ireland' in Vincenzo Ruggiero, Mick Ryan and Joe Sim, *Western European Penal Systems: A Critical Anatomy,* London Sage, 1995

Truxes, Thomas M. *Irish-American Trade, 1660-1783*, Cambridge University Press, 1988

Van Der Zee, Henri and Barbara. *William and Mary*, London, Macmillan, 1973

Wagner, Heinrich. 'Near Eastern and African Connections with the Celtic World', in R. O'Driscoll (ed), *The Celtic Consciousness*, Portlaoise/Edinburgh, Dolmen Press/ Mountrath, 1982: pp. 51-67

Warm, David. 'The Jews of Northern Ireland', in Paul Hainsworth (ed). *Divided Society: Ethnic Minorities and Racism in Northern Ireland*, London, Pluto Press, 1998: 222-239

Watson, Anna Manwah and McKnight, Eleanor. 'Race and Ethnicity in Northern Ireland: the Chinese Community, in Paul Hainsworth (ed). *Divided Society: Ethnic Minorities and Racism in Northern Ireland*, London, Pluto Press, 1998: 127-151

Webber, Frances. *Crimes of Arrival: Immigrants and Asylum-seekers in the new Europe*, London, Statewatch, 1996

Weir, Anthony. *Early Ireland: a Field Guide*, Belfast, Blackstaff Press, 1980

Wittke, Carl. *The Irish in America*, New York, Russell and Russell, 1970

Wood, Forrest G. *Black Scare: the Racist Response to Emancipation and Reconstruction*, Berkeley, University of California Press, 1970

Woodson, Carter G. and Wesley, Charles H. *The Negro in Our History*, Washington, D.C., The Associated Publishers Inc., 1970

Words in the House of Sound, Cape Town, District Six Museum, 2000

Index